"Some editors are failed writers, but so are most writers."

T.S. Eliot

POD PEOPLE

PEOPLE

BEATING THE PRINT-ON-DEMAND STIGMA

A GUIDE
by
JEREMY ROBINSON

BREAKNECK
BOOKS

Published by Breakneck Books (USA)
www.breakneckbooks.com

First printing, July 2006

Printed in the United States of America.

Visit Jeremy Robinson on the World Wide Web at:
www.jeremyrobinsononline.com.

For all the fans of *The Didymus Contingency*. Without your support, a book based on my publishing success could never have been written.

ACKNOWLEDGEMENTS

First and foremost, I must again acknowledge the fans of *The Didymus Contingency*. I know from the many letters I have received that it is primarily thanks to you spreading the word about the book that it received any measure of success. I hope you continue to follow my career through the next book and beyond.

I'd also like to thank David Rising, a fellow Lulu.com author who, early on, taught me some tips about marketing on Amazon.com. Without his guidance, I'm not sure what fate would have befallen my first novel.

I must also thank Lulu.com, who made the publication of *The Didymus Contingency* possible. Beyond that, you have been a tremendous support and have offered excellent service to me. The amazing kickstart to my writing career was made possible by you.

No author stands alone. I'd like to thank my close group of loyal supporters, friends and family. Stan {AOE} Tremblay, Elizabeth Tremblay, Frank Ferris, Kathy Crisp, Matthew, Sandi and Cole Robinson, Frank and Donna Robinson (mom and dad), Josh, Ana and Eli Robinson, Roger and Cathie Brodeur, James Rollins, Karen Cooper, Aaron and Stasia Brodeur and Thor.

As always, special thanks go to my wife, Hilaree, for her tireless devotion to her family and for giving me the time to write. To my daughter, Aquila, you continue to inspire me everyday. I love you both.

AUTHOR'S NOTE:

Before getting started I would like to explain that this book is not a technical manual. While I give tips on cover design and software to use in cover creation, I do not teach how to use the software or how to create good designs. Those subjects would require several books and a few good instructors to learn sufficiently. The same is true for the other technical subjects involved in the POD process, such as interior layout using Word, writing skills and POD service requirements (image size, spine calculations, ISBN issues, etc.) There are books that cover these subjects in detail and any information needed to properly format your images and text should be available from your POD service. If not...time to get a new POD service!

STIGMA BUSTER STAMPS

Any time you see this stamp at the beginning of a chapter or section, you should pay close attention. The information following a Stigma Buster stamp is especially useful for setting yourself, and your book, apart from the rest of the print-on-demand (POD) world and for breaking free of the stigma that dooms most POD books to literary oblivion.

TABLE OF CONTENTS

1

WHO THE HECK IS JEREMY ROBINSON?

While I'm sure everyone would like to hear my childhood stories about setting traps for neighborhood kids, almost drowning twice and rescuing a girl in my one and only fight, I'll save that for my memoirs when I'm old and gray and have a few NY Times bestsellers under my belt. Though, I will mention that to rescue the girl, I did have to fight two bullies at once...and I won.

My writing career began about ten years ago. Before that I had dabbled in writing, taking classes here and there, but never considered it a career option. I was an illustrator and my first job was a comic book...which I was also asked to write. The book came out great and I began writing comics as well as illustrating them. I worked on a few indie books, *Ralph*, *Klaus* and *Soldier of God*. And then I was offered a position writing and illustrating a comic book series. This wasn't a one shot deal, it was an entire series, written and illustrated by me. The characters and basic story had been created, but the rest was mine to develop. It was a great time in my career, and remains some of my best illustration work. Then the indie publisher (note I'm leaving out names here) announced they would also be publishing pornography. Not wanting to have my work associated with a company like this, I quit. And it was because of this that my eyes were opened. In the mid-nineties the comic book industry was at a low point. And in their desperation for sales they started filling pages with mostly naked women and a lot less story. I became disenchanted with the whole industry.

My focus morphed from comic books to movies and I began learning to write screenplays. I was a voracious writer, writing and rewriting screenplays for years. Some screenplays got total makeovers two or three times. Then the time came. I was ready for the big move—Los Angeles. My wife and I headed west from New Hampshire, about as far from home in the continental United States as you can go. We arrived in L.A. with little money, no jobs and no place to live. Within a month we had an apartment, jobs and I landed an internship with an agency in Bel Air. A short time later the agency connected me with a literary manager who signed me on after reading my screenplays. Things progressed quickly. I had a screenplay in development (the screenplay version of *The*

Didymus Contingency, simply titled *Didymus*), I had another screenplay optioned and two more getting rave reviews (though no takers) at the major studios. In one month I wrote and sold *The Screenplay Workbook,* my first published book. But after only two and a half years Hollywood began to lose its luster. In fact, I had written my first novel (*The Didymus Contingency*) within a year of being there.

This wasn't a sudden realization like it was with comic books. It was a gradual realization that Hollywood incorporated more smoke and mirrors on a daily basis than Copperfield has in a lifetime. The industry felt like a permanent chain yanking festival and no one gave a rip about you unless you could make them money. There are, of course, exceptions to this rule (those brave honest souls who can stand the duality) but I am not one of them.

It was during this transitional stage that I took a chance with my favorite author, James Rollins. I sent him an e-mail explaining that I was interested in adapting some of his books into screenplays. His answer was kind and honest. He explained that he was already working with a screenwriter and that the rights to many of the books had been bought. After another few e-mails about his books in general I worked up the courage and asked him to read this novel I'd written: *The Didymus Contingency.* To my utter amazement, he agreed.

Three months later I received an e-mail exclaiming the virtues of my book from my favorite author. I was stunned. The blurb he provided then is the one now gracing the cover of the book. It was

James' encouragement, kindness and honesty (all of which I had yet to discover in Hollywood) that got me thinking about switching gears again.

It wasn't long after this that my wife and I made the cross country trek back to the east coast. I wrote two more screenplays during the summer of my return. I think they're both great, but have never attempted to do anything with them. Since then I've been writing novels. I'm working on my fifth right now.

But how and why did I eventually choose the POD route for *The Didymus Contingency*? I never tried taking the book out to traditional publishers because it was both too Christian and too mainstream. The Christian aspects made the book a risk to mass market publishers and the violence, substance abuse and light cursing broke the CBA (Christian Booksellers Association) rules, making it taboo for Christian publishers. I knew this ahead of time and held the book in reserve while I continued writing and attempted to go the traditional route of finding a publisher or agent—endless query letters. I got a few nibbles here and there, enough to keep me feeling depressed, but not enough to kill my motivation.

I began to feel the urge to try something different. The idea of self-publishing entered my mind. I'd heard of a few people selling enough of their own books to get noticed. I e-mailed James Rollins, who I'd been in touch with regularly over the years and asked his advice. I wanted to self-publish *The Didymus Contingency* because I thought people would buy it and like it, and I had no plans to send it to traditional publishers. He agreed with my assessment that it would be a hard sell, but that people would enjoy it. It was settled. I was going to self-publish.

I looked into pricing and my hopes were dashed into microbe sized pieces. Self-publishing was going to run me thousands of dollars. I was a poor starving artist with more credit card debt than the nation of Chad! Self-publishing was no longer an option. A last resort web search brought me across a website that described this strange new technology, Print-On-Demand. It was supposed to be affordable, and compared to traditional self-publishing it was. But it would still cost me well over $1000. Much too high for me. Reinvigorated, I looked deeper into this print-on-demand thing and after finding all sorts of publishers outside my price range and asking for contracts, I discovered Lulu.com. I immediately saw the value in them. I would control everything. There was no contract and I retained all rights. It was easy to use, easy to navigate and the support community was excellent. I'm not being paid by Lulu to say any of this. It's simply the truth. They allow people with the right skills to produce professional books for a fraction of the price other PODs request.

So this was it. This was my choice. After two months of editing my book several times, creating a cover, laying out the interior and trying to understand everything I needed to do after the book was published, I paid my $150 and released the book globally. It was a great feeling. Sales were immediate. I was on top of the world.

Then a week later, reality.

My friends and family had bought the book. No one was left. There were no sales. And I came to the realization that I was totally unprepared. I was so far out of the loop I didn't know the loop existed. I began scouring Lulu's message boards for advice. And lucky me, I found some. I found tips on marketing at Amazon and other online retailers from a few knowledgeable Lulu authors, though primarily from one author, David Rising. I followed David's advice and combined it with new efforts of my own. I created a large mailing list that went beyond just friends and family to include everyone I had even a slight relationship with. I wrote up and distributed press releases. I scheduled book signings. I sent my book out for reviews. All of this should have been done ahead of time, or at least prepared ahead of time, but now I was playing catch up.

Lucky for me, my wife and I both work at home taking care of a man with disabilities. This meant I had full-time hours to combat the problems I now faced, and I did so for two weeks straight.

Things began to change. The book slowly started to sell, and the buyers were complete strangers! My anxiety began to wane, but I knew my goal of 10,000 copies sold was far from attainable. Then the unbelievable took place. Within three days my sales rank on Amazon jumped to 3000. At the same time, my sales rank on Barnes&Noble.com jumped to 92—a bestseller! The same was happening in Canada and the U.K. as well. It seemed like all of a sudden people everywhere were buying my book. What was most amazing about this is that I hadn't spent a dime on marketing.

The next day I ran to check my stats. Amazon remained strong, but my Barnes&Noble rank had jumped to 72. An even better bestseller, and I was now beating two out of four of Dan Brown's books! Relieved that the book was still selling, I sat down to check my e-mail. At the time I rarely received much e-mail and expected to see the same result. Then I saw it, "Receiving Message 1 of 1."

The message popped up on my screen and I read the e-mail address. It was from a literary agency that I knew by name, from an agent on my list of agents I wished I could have but had no chance of attracting. This is true. My jaw dropped as I read the e-mail.

The agent had seen my book online and wanted to read a copy. A few hours later I was speaking to him on the phone. Two days later he had a copy in hand. Three days after that he called me and asked to represent me. I now have one of the best agents in the business at one of the largest, most reputable agencies in the world. All because of a tiny little POD book I put together myself. If you're reading this book, you know that this alone is a wonderful success for any author.

Since this time, we have yet to sell the domestic rights to the book (I knew it would be a hard sell and it was for the very reasons I feared), but European countries are eating it up and we now have several foreign translations in the works. This brings you to the current day. I'm still working on my fifth novel. My agent is looking at my other three, deciding which to release next, and I'm waiting for the next big phone call. It still feels like a lifetime away, but I know I'm closer than ever.

In this book I'm going to tell you everything I learned in those first few months. You'll find out everything I did to gain all those sales. I'll show you the mistakes I made that probably cost me sales. And I'll let you know how I've maintained sales over the past few months. It's my hope that *POD People* will help you boost sales, improve your chances of getting noticed and help you avoid the mistakes I made along the way. Best of all, you'll learn how to best avoid the POD stigma.

2

WHY POD?

Since POD became available and popular, the world has become inundated by publications that would have never before seen the light of day. Some deserve to be printed, some don't. Few become wonderful successes, while most fall to the wayside to be forgotten without sparking any more interest than the original manuscript did. As independent publishers, we have been given the opportunity to see our work published, listed on sites like Amazon and available in bookstores.

POD has given hope to the thousands of writers struggling to get noticed, longing to be plucked from the slush pile, cleaned off and handed a six figure contract. We all want the same thing, to be professional writers, to be paid to do what we love. For many,

POD has been an alternate means of accomplishing this goal (it was for me).

In the past, those who wanted to self-publish had to find a printer, pay for thousands of books up front, distribute and list their books online. And most of the time the book covers were limited by printing costs. Books with no cover image and simple black and white designs were common. Not so with POD. Now we have full color, vivid covers and the ability to be listed online with little effort.

POD has provided so much for writers that we infrequently stop to consider if it is the right choice. It's an affordable way to get published and get noticed, and provides authors with the ability to say, "Look! My book is published!"

But before any author takes up self-publishing or POD publishing the question needs to be asked: why? What is your reason, your motivation, your goal behind printing the book yourself? Let's dissect the most common reasons authors choose the POD route.

MONEY

This is actually a common reason. Many authors have an unwavering faith in their own work. They believe their book will be the next *Da Vinci Code* and that Michael Crichton can't write to save his life. Admit it. You feel like this at times, don't you?

Picture this: You've just sent your manuscript to a publisher, and not just any publisher, but the one you've researched and have decided would be the one to publish your next twenty books. Three months have past and then you get it, a letter in the mail. The handwriting, your own, immediately tells you that the letter is your very own self-addressed stamped envelope that you enclosed with your impeccably printed manuscript. Now your hands are sweating and the ham and cheese sandwich you ate for lunch begins to make you ill. You know that receiving a SASE is never a good thing—if they wanted to publish your book they'd call. But the envelope is thicker than one sheet of paper could account for.

Maybe they've enclosed a contract?

Maybe it's an invitation to meet with them?

Maybe they wrote several pages about how great your book is?

You bring the letter inside, sit at the kitchen table, rip it open and start reading. You have yet to take a breath since opening the mail box. You read the first sentence three times before it makes any sense: *Sorry, but your manuscript does not fit our current needs.*

Without reading the rest of the letter, you realize the mystery second page is simply the title page of your manuscript. At the bottom right corner is a hand written note in green ink: *I thought your story was interesting but the characters need further development and the descriptive text was bland at times. Good luck! – Signed, Hard Working Editor.*

Okay, now be honest. If you've been earnestly trying to get your novel published, chances are you've received a letter something like this. I know I have. Your first thought is probably something like: Bland? Bland! I know more about writing than this editor ever will. At which point you might choose to spew a string of obscenities, burn the letter or send the editor a scathing e-mail.

Why would you do that? Because you are a professional writer, better than any of those hacks on the bestseller list and that editor is just too dumb to see your genius. You could be making oodles of money if only someone would publish your book. Then you hear about POD, about how affordable it is, about how your book will be on Amazon, about how that Jeremy Robinson guy got an agent and sold the foreign book rights...and he's a hack too!

A plan starts to congeal in your mind. You picture sales—100,000 in the first year. Then you do the math. You can sell your 250 page paperback for $20 and people will buy it, it's that good. That makes your royalty somewhere around $4 a book. 4 x 100,000 = $400,000! You'd make more money in one year than you have at your current job in the last ten years combined!

Stop.

Breathe.

Think.

Making enough money to live off of through the publication of a POD book is an unrealistic goal. The average number of sales for a POD book is 500...total, and I often wonder if that is an exaggeration. POD is not a money making machine. *The Didymus Contingency* has sold and continues to sell wonderfully. But I'm not paying my bills with the money I've made. I'm not buying boats or cars or fancy, riding lawn mowers. I've made enough money to reinvest in my writing via a laptop, a few books and a few more Christmas presents than normal, that's it.

These are all great things for me, but for those of you who imagine POD as a way to get rich quick; my laptop seems more like a door prize than the grand prize. My advice is this, if you expect to make a living off your POD book, think again and then, perhaps try to make your money some other way...the stock market perhaps.

EXPERIENCE

There are some people who recognize that having your work in print and read by the public is one of the best ways to learn how you need to improve. Every guide or instruction book about writing insists, "Don't ask your family or friends to read your manuscript because they won't be honest." It's really become a writing advice cliché.

What POD provides is a way to have people read your book and let you know what they think. And will they ever. Remember these people *paid* for your book *and* they're total strangers. If they hated it, you're going to hear about it. At the same time, people who enjoy your work are likely to let you know why as well. Since publishing *The Didymus Contingency* I have quickly learned how I need to improve and what I'm doing right. I've never had a better learning experience with writing in my life.

Not only will you learn to improve your writing, you'll also learn valuable lessons about the publishing industry. As a self-publisher you'll be functioning not only as author, but also as publisher, editor, designer, marketer and public relations. You will experience every facet of the publishing world for yourself. I have a new found respect for editors' abilities to find typos. I understand how much work goes into marketing a book and getting the public's attention. These are all important realizations because you will be working with these people in the future. It will help you relate and understand problems. It will improve your relationships with future editors and publishers because you'll know what they're doing. When my first book, *The Screenplay Workbook*, was published by Lone Eagle Publishing, I sometimes felt frustrated by timeframes, book changes and design modifications. Luckily, my editor was very forthcoming and set my mind at ease. But the singular reason for my confusion was a lack of knowledge. Through the printing and marketing of *The Didymus Contingency*, I have a much more well-rounded knowledge base in the publishing world and I find myself less confused and frustrated.

If you're looking to learn about your skills and potential as a writer, or about the publishing industry, there are few better ways to do so than through self-publishing a POD book. There can be a few problems, however. If you suspect your writing needs improvement and you want honest opinions, make the print version of your book as low in price as you possibly can by giving yourself zero royalties. I'd also recommend making the downloadable e-book version free. Charging full price may result in stronger negative reviews because people may feel ripped off. If you want honest opinions (and you do) a low cost book or free download will avoid creating bias based on price. You'll quickly learn what mistakes exist and will have the opportunity to improve your book before taking it to publishers.

While this kind of education is an excellent reason for trying out POD, it is an aspect I hadn't considered before my own POD experience. I'm happy to have discovered this welcome side effect but it was not my personal motivation for self-publishing. This brings me to my third and final reason for choosing to publish via POD.

EXPOSURE

One of the options a POD publisher has is to take their book global. What this means is that your book will be available, not only at your POD of choice (Lulu.com, IUniverse, Publish America, etc.) but also at online retailers around the world. Your book will sell in Japan, Germany, England, Canada and more. Online stores like Amazon, Barnes&Noble, Wal-Mart, Buy.com, Target and Books-A-Million will carry your book online. In the virtual realm, your book will be as available as any put out by the publishing industry's big guns.

Not only will your book be visible, but through this visibility you will have the opportunity to sell large numbers of books. Before you tackle me and shout, "You said making money was a bad reason to self-publish!" let me explain. By reducing the amount of royalty you make on each book you decrease the amount of money you make, but you simultaneously increase the chances someone might buy your book!

The end goal here can be accomplished in two ways.

1. Publishers tend to take notice of self-published books that sell 10,000 copies. Why? Because even many traditionally published books don't sell that many copies. Some don't even sell 2000 copies. What this sales number says to publishers is that A) the book is good, B) the author knows how to market himself, and C) with some advertising dollars behind the book, it could be a money-maker for them too.

Granted, selling 10,000 copies is an undertaking of enormous proportions that takes time and money beyond the resources of the common struggling author, myself included. However, this was my goal when I began the POD process. Will I reach this goal at my current rate of sales? Yes, which is wonderful, but it's going to take much longer than I had anticipated, and probably longer than would garner the interest of a publisher.

Luckily for me there are other ways in which POD books get noticed. Because my book is sold via Lulu.com's global package, my book is available all over the world. The results, simply from being listed on Amazon's worldwide sites, have been staggering. I have been contacted by publishers from countries like Spain, Germany, Bulgaria, Romania and Demark, several of which I now have contracts with. These contacts came about with no effort on my part. They found me because the book was visible.

Perhaps the most amazing benefit for me has been signing with a top literary agency. This is how I understand the process unfolded. My book is listed on Amazon. During its first month online the book became a Barnes&Noble.com bestseller and was selling at a healthy rate on Amazon as well. People who had bought my book also bought a book by Joel C. Rosenberg, a NY Times bestselling author who happens to be represented by my new agency. This created a "People who have bought this book have also bought..." listing on one of Rosenberg's bestselling book's Amazon pages (*The Ezekiel Option*). At the time, *The Ezekiel Option* was around 25 on the Amazon bestseller list and our now mutual agent was visiting the Amazon list to get the latest number. While at the page he looked at the "People who have also bought..." list, saw my book and followed the link. He saw the synopsis, read the many positive reviews, found my website and made contact.

All of this happened simply because my book was visible online. It had exposure and it got noticed. It had nothing to do with my sales figures. He didn't even know the book was a Barnes&Noble.com bestseller.

If your book is well written and your cover design is professional then the possibility of getting noticed online is good. I've never had more interest in my writing and I haven't written a single query letter, or looked in my *Writer's Market*, or researched an agency in over a year.

I firmly believe that if you are ready, POD publishing is one of the best new ways to get noticed by the publishing world.

3

ARE *YOU* READY?

If you're still with me after having your get-rich-quick POD dreams crushed, good. It means you're in this for the right reasons. But there is more to consider before taking the POD plunge.

Here are some of the questions you'll need to ask yourself: What am I going to do for my cover design? Do I know how to layout the interior of a book? Do I know how to write effective copy for the back cover of my book? You need to know the answers to a staggering amount of questions (and your answers better be "yes" to all of the above), but these are not the question I'm asking now. We're not there yet. There is still one, very important question that is the penultimate query every writer needs to answer before changing their title from "writer" to "author." I'll phrase the question in several different ways so there can be no miscommunication.

Are you a good writer?

Is your writing professional?

Have you had anything published, ever?

Can you swear on your Aunt Beatrice's grave that your book is better than 90% of the myriad other POD titles swamping the market?

I mean no insult to the POD community, but we all need to be honest. A large majority of POD books are just plain awful. Cover designs are...well, they're not designed. Interior layout is often neglected. Editing, the second most important aspect of the writing process, is left by the wayside like a leprous dog. This is not just my opinion, but the opinion of the general public—our customers. It really doesn't matter what you think, it matters what your readers think. And as more and more unready authors slap covers on their 150 page novel, price it at $20 and sell it to the public, the more the public's opinion of POD books will sour.

Many POD books have been listed on Amazon, and many do well there. But what happens to sales when someone posts a review that reveals your book is self-published, and more than that, it is a POD book? I've seen this happen to two different POD books in the past year, and they weren't necessarily bad books or even bad reviews. But the simple statement of, "This is a POD self-published book," killed sales instantly. This reveals how strong the public aversion to self-published and POD books really is, and the only way it will ever change is if the POD community, as a whole, publishes better work.

So, are you ready? This is an all important question for every single POD author/publisher to consider and answer honestly! If the reading public considers all POD books as garbage, which they're close to doing, then POD publishing will go the way of the Velociraptor and no amount of Crichton-like ingenuity will bring it back to life.

I understand that from a POD perspective, having thousands of authors publishing a few hundred books is great business. That's quick, easy money. But to sustain that business a good number of books need to be good. And some even need to be great! In the end, this is the only thing that will not only sustain the business, but grow the business. What happens to Ford when tires start blowing out? Sales tank. What happens when you eat at a restaurant and find some kind of nastiness in your food? You stop eating there. What happens when you give a few POD titles a chance and they're all awful? You stop buying POD books!

WHAT TO DO ABOUT IT

I'm sure plenty of readers are now miffed, but hear me out. I am not telling you to never self-publish. I am not telling you that if you're not ready now, you never will be. I'm not even telling you that 90% of POD authors should give up and accept their day jobs as their permanent lot in life. That's not how I think. I can't even fathom saying something like that.

What I am saying is that a vast majority of POD authors need to improve. Take classes. Write daily. Read up on the subject. Do research. Improve grammar and memorize a dictionary. Learn to take and understand criticism. Whatever it takes to improve your writing, do it. Having a successful writing career might take ten years, but I swear to you it will take much longer if you don't put all your time and effort into improving as a writer, especially if you publish something prematurely and gain a reputation as a poor writer.

There are several ways to do this. Write short stories and submit them to magazines. Graciously accept any advice they give if you're rejected. Comments from a professional editor should be considered equal in worth to gold to an amateur author. Join serious writers' groups that give honest critiques. Join online writers' groups. Take some college level classes. Or, as I mentioned in the first chapter, make your POD free and let it be known that you want critiques. Every reader that is not biased (family/friend) who provides you with commentary on your book should be welcomed as a dear friend. It is they who improve your writing. And that is the only way to climb the literary ladder.

Beyond improving our writing skills there are a few other things to develop. Cover design is at the top of the list. As an illustrator I cringe at the majority of cover designs found at my POD of choice, Lulu.com. Most people, me included, choose Lulu because the price is right and we don't have to pay for a cover. We can make our own. This is incredibly freeing...and dangerous. If you're like most starving artists, the idea of paying for a cover design, let alone anything at all, is ludicrous. But nothing will kill book sales faster than a bad cover.

Cover designs made from MS Word Art or collaged in a paint program from downloaded web images scream, "This is self published!" A bad cover also communicates to the shopper that you don't care about your work. A sloppy cover is almost always followed up by sloppy writing. When you go to a job interview you don't wear ripped blue jeans and an old T-shirt. You wear something nice, heck, you might even go out and *buy* something. Why? Because you know first impressions are all people need to make a judgment. If you dress lazily, you're probably lazy. If your cover is a mess or boring, so is your writing. It's harsh to be judged this way, but I feel it's generally an accurate judgment. Knowing this ahead of time should convince you to put as much effort into your cover as you do your writing. At the very least find a design savvy friend to help. At best, hire a graphic designer. The few hundred dollars you spend on the cover will be paid back in sales. Even if you have a truly amazing book, save for an entire year to buy a good cover if you have to. If you rush the process by allowing your book to be published with a sub-par cover, your book will be passed by faster than a grandma driving on the highway.

Interior design is also important, though not as challenging as cover design. If you are intrepid and resourceful enough, it is possible to do the entire layout within Word. Just make sure that you are not satisfied until your book's interior looks as good as any other book published today.

That is the advice I give every single time an author asks me what they need to do to be a successful POD author: make your book, in every way, as good as or better than the traditionally published books in your genre. Before releasing your book to the world at large, try this: print a single copy of the book and bring it to the bookstore. Find the section of the store that holds similar books (being a POD, your book is most likely a 6x9 trade paperback, so look for a table of 6x9 books). Place your book with the others, step back and see if it sticks out like a sore thumb. Be harsh. Be a critic. Ask the opinion of the store's customers. Better yet, ask the store employees what they think. Send the book to a professional editor and make certain the story and grammar are brilliant. Find every possible judge you can and milk them for all they're worth.

Only after you've been completely honest with yourself can you be ready to become a successful POD author. Make it a habit. Become your own harshest critic. I know I am. I've found design flaws and typos in my book since it was published and I kick myself for it so often that I'm less likely to do it again. If you're serious about being an author, about being noticed and about supporting the POD community with quality work then take your time, learn the skills you need and don't be satisfied until the book is 100%.

Otherwise the POD boat is going to sink and take all of us with it.

WORDS OF WARNING
WRITING GROUPS

Writing groups can be both a blessing and a curse. There are some that are run well and serve each and every member with honest critique. But, and perhaps this is just my personal experience, many simply consume time and energy like a mutant leech. It's hard to tell if you're getting good advice in some groups because many writers think that they're the culmination of the world's literary knowledge. No matter what they read, they think its drivel...everything except for their own work of course. In many writers' groups, everything that is read is torn to pieces by so many different people with different opinions it's impossible to sort out what is good advice and what is bad. On top of that, many writers' group attendees are novice writers and if you're past that stage, your time in the group will be spent editing other people's work. The time you spend editing other people's work is time wasted. You could have been *writing!* Try to stick with smaller writing groups made up of published authors or those seriously pursuing a career.

Here's an example of a writers' group gone bad. Before publishing *The Didymus Contingency* I decided to let an online writers' group take a peek. Little did I know that this was really a voracious pack of hypercritics. A group of about ten told me that every aspect of the book was rubbish; the cover, the cover text, the writing and the concept. And they did so angrily. I was discouraged for about a week but soon realized the kind of people I was talking to—bitter writers. Avoid them like the plague and ignore their comments. They assured me the book wouldn't sell a single copy, but alas (or should I say fortunately), they were wrong.

Join writers' groups, but pay close attention to the criticisms you hear. If they seem too harsh or unwarranted, find another group...or better yet, start one yourself. Oh, and please, don't be a bitter writer. We've all been rejected as a writer. No need to take that out on someone else.

4

WHAT COMES NEXT?

The process of designing a cover, laying out the interior and editing your writing are all important steps in the journey to becoming
a bestselling POD author. However, they are not the subjects I'll
be covering in detail. I'll provide tips and hints, but most people go
to school to learn graphic design. There are volumes of books written on graphic design and writing technique and everything you
need to know about putting your book together at a POD should
be available on their website. Each one is different and since I've
only published through Lulu.com, I won't pretend to be an expert
on the other POD services. As for Lulu technical details, I learned
everything I needed to know about publishing my book via
Lulu.com through the Lulu FAQs, message boards and help
guides. I suggest you start your research there.

What you should have at this point is a finished book with a brilliant cover that has been professionally edited. Unless you are publishing for feedback, you should not have made your book available to the public yet. There is much more to be done before your book's debut.

But before you get started on what comes next, you need to be mentally, financially and emotionally prepared. You've got to be committed to the project and see your book through to the end. By the time you're finished putting your book together, you might think the hardest part is over. But you'd be wrong. The road ahead is full of potholes and frost heaves waiting to steer you in the wrong direction and send your book careening into oblivion.

Your next two separate yet intertwined steps toward the goal of becoming a bestselling POD author are book reviews and author blurbs—stamps of approval from folks who know better.

STAMPS OF APPROVAL

It's Saturday morning and you're thinking about going to a movie. If you live in New England (like I do) this is the main event of your day and might be proceeded by dinner out. If you live in Los Angeles (which I did) you'll probably go to a movie, then lunch, then Universal Studios, then dinner and top it all of with a night of clubbing. Whatever your speed or preference you'll probably do one thing before deciding which movie to see...

You'll read reviews. You'll look for quotes by respected directors or actors. Their opinions are valuable. People like to be informed before spending hard earned money. We regularly use other people's opinions to assure ourselves that something might be worth. In particular, people who are in positions to know better. Whether it's two thumbs up from Ebert or a quote from Mel Gibson, we pay attention.

The same is true with book buying. I may not always read book reviews in magazines and newspapers but you better believe I read the text on the book cover. But reviews aren't everything. A good review simply reassures me that other people enjoyed the book. An author blurb, on the other hand, tells me what kind of book I'm holding. I'm a science based action/adventure fanatic. If I pick up a book and see a blurb from Douglas Preston, Michael Crichton or James Rollins, chances are I'm going to buy that book. A quote from one of those authors tells me two things. 1) The book is in a genre that causes me to salivate like Pavlov's Chihuahua. 2) The writing is good (established authors wouldn't put their reputation on the line by supporting drivel). Seeing an author blurb from a writer I already like not only makes me more interested in buying the book, but I'm also likely to go out and find every other novel by my newly discovered novelist.

Reviews and author blurbs are extremely important for new writers. Here's what you need to know.

REVIEWS

This is where I almost blew it. I was ignorant to the review process and as a result missed out on several reviews that would have helped tremendously and still would. Many of the large reviewers like NY Times, Kirkus Reviews, Foreword Magazine, etc., will only review your book *before* it is published!

Here's how it works. When your book is ready to go, set a publication date three to four months away. That means if it is December 1 when your book is ready to go, set a publication date for March 1 or April 1. This gives you a good period of time to approach the larger review houses and increases your chance of getting reviewed. But don't wait too long. Most reviews take about three months to go through so they will be published around the same date as your release. See how the timing works out? Having the review in hand before the book is published also lets you add those wonderful quotes to the back cover of the book, establishing a positive reputation for your book before it's made a single sale.

Some people ignore the importance of these reviews and that is a terrible mistake. Here's why. Book reviews are not printed in a mysterious realm only seen by the author of the book. They are read by people...and typically by people interested in books, specifically librarians, book stores, publishers and agents! The people who have the ability to sell and purchase your book to more people than you could ever imagine read book reviews all the time.

A note on libraries: A relatively unknown fact to many POD authors is that librarians depend on reviews for stocking their shelves and often purchase multiple copies. I've had my book placed in more than a couple of libraries around the country and I had nothing to do with it! Positive reviews make this possible. What's great about libraries is that unlike bookstores, they don't care if a book is returnable or not. There are 9,211 public libraries in the United States, not including the thousands of school and university libraries. The potential sales from libraries alone are staggering. It's a great resource you can only cultivate by getting good reviews.

Having a few good reviews from well known review houses can jumpstart your sales even before the book is released. Big publishers know this too and they proceed the same way. It may be utterly painful for you to hold off releasing your book, but ultimately, if your goal is to succeed, you should at least try to get some pre-release reviews.

But that's not where the review process stops! No, there are countless smaller review houses that post reviews on websites and publish reviews via newsletters. They might not be as well known as the major review houses, but they increase your book's visibility and help garner sales. And you can pursue them throughout the life of your book. I've had about four reviews done every three months. Each time reviews come out, sales go up. Granted, they have to be good reviews, but if you were honest with yourself in the beginning and made sure your book was perfect, good reviews are inevitable. I have yet to receive a bad review for *The Didymus Contingency* and each positive review has increased my sales.

After your book is published you can't add reviews to the cover without putting out a second edition (often for a fee) but you can quote them on your Amazon and Barnes&Noble.com pages. As a POD author/publisher, Amazon is the #1 place to sell a lot of books. The more positive reviews you can put on the site from official reviewers, the better.

Basically, don't stop looking for reviews until there is no one left to review your book. Each one pays off.

What you'll need: Book reviews are free. If a reviewer (other than Kirkus) charges for a review, they're probably not legit and you should avoid them. Kirkus does have a review service you have to pay for. It's called Kirkus Discoveries. The reason for this is that Kirkus does not review self-published book (for free). Paying a steep $350 gets your book reviewed by Kirkus Discoveries. A good review still gives you bragging rights, but I'm not sure $350 is a fair price. I chose not to pursue this option, though others have.

What you will have to pay for is copies of your book and postage. Don't even consider asking a reviewer if you can e-mail them a copy of the book (unless they specify that e-books are acceptable). If you do, they will most likely not ask for your book because it marks you as an amateur. You costs for the review process could range between $100 and $200 total depending on how many reviews you try to get and how you mail your book (media mail, first class, priority, etc.). Of course, if you include a letter or other promotion materials, you cannot send the book via media mail. Plain old first class is fine. Priority is a little overkill because it's going to be a few months before your book gets reviewed. My review costs for *The Didymus Contingency* are just under $100 and I've got eight great reviews to show for it.

Now you're wondering how on earth to find book reviewers. There are a few simple ways.

1. This is the most obvious. Do a Google search for "Book Reviewers" and you'll come up with a bunch.

2. Visit the bookstore, pick up a paperback and look at the back cover and first few pages. They're usually filled with book reviews from websites. That's how I found all of my review sources.

3. Save yourself all sorts of time by skipping 1. and 2. and visit my favorite review site, The Midwest Book Review. Alone, they are a great review house, giving preference to self-published titles and being read by the majority of libraries, but they also provide a detailed list of other reviewers. Rather than copy their list and use up more paper, here is the web address for their review list:
http://www.midwestbookreview.com/links/othr_rev.htm

That webpage is pure gold, people. Use it.

AUTHOR BLURBS

Like the book reviews, this absolutely needs to be done months in advance. These are the quotes you not only want on your back cover, but on your front cover as well. More than anything else, author blurbs sell books. As I've mentioned, long before I decided to give POD a whirl with *The Didymus Contingency*, James Rollins agreed to read the manuscript and liked it enough to provide a blurb. In fact, he liked it enough that he now reads all of my books!

What many people say when they hear this story is, "Wow, you're so lucky to have him as a friend." What they don't realize is that when I contacted him, I was a complete stranger. I was a screenwriter and he was my favorite author. I completely expected to be turned down, but I wasn't! The point is, you just need to ask. Sure, the author you ask might say no. It happens to me all the time. But many authors say yes. And as a POD author, there is no better way to legitimize your book to readers than to have another, established author give your book a stamp of approval. That's why James Rollins' books have blurbs from Clive Cussler, and Cussler's books have blurbs from Douglas Preston, and so on. An author blurb also lets you tap into an established fan base. I know for a fact (because they e-mail me) that several Rollins fans have bought my book simply because he recommended it.

You need to contact authors for author blurbs even before your book is bound and printed. Some authors are willing to read a book while it's still a manuscript. Expect to be disappointed if you only give an author three months to read and review your book. They're busy people and get tons of books to read from eager writers. If they agree, send your book immediately. But don't be surprised if the author still doesn't get back to you by your publication date. Even though I'm "in" with James Rollins, it sometimes still takes him six months to get to a book I send him.

Contacting an author can be a challenge. Many list their e-mail address in their books and on their websites. If they do, they're your best bet. By making themselves readily available to the reading public, it means that they're generally more friendly and are probably used to being contacted by other authors. The traditional route to contact an author is to send a letter to the author, c/o their publisher. This is a much slower process but can still create results. About six months ago I was contacted by Greg Vilk, author of *Golem*. He asked me to read his book and provide a blurb. I was flattered that people were now coming to me for blurbs, but I also knew he needed bigger guns backing him up. So I recommended Stel Pavlou, author of *Decipher*. Both books had a similar element (Golem). I had no connection with Pavlou and he didn't have a website. So Greg sent him a letter via his publisher and voilá, he now has a blurb from Pavlou for his book. And I guarantee readers who enjoyed *Decipher* will now strongly consider *Golem* simply because Pavlou gave it a thumbs-up.

There is no list of author e-mails, no directory to find them. For this part you have to do the running around and research on your own. But it's not difficult. Go to the bookstore and find your genre. Pick out authors in your genre and read the "About the Author" section. If an author has an e-mail address or website listed, write it down! You're half way there. You can also try searching for them online. At the very least you are likely to find their publisher's website and can find out where to send your letter.

This is an opportunity that the majority of POD authors let slip by without even considering it. But you better be ready for rejection. You're asking professional authors their opinion of your book. They might not like it! And they might tell you why. It can be a huge ego crusher to be critiqued by your favorite authors, so do yourself a favor...be honest about your writing! Have I said that enough yet?

WORDS OF WARNING
AUTHOR BLURBS

As discussed, author blurbs can help sell books. But, like I said, authors might not like your work, and might tell you so. Being egocentric writers, our instinct is to fight back. We suddenly feel our views of the author change. They transform from author supreme into critic from Hades. This is the natural response of many writers and it is WRONG!

- Do not send the offending author an angry e-mail.
- Do not send them a dead cat in the mail.
- Do not change your opinions about their books (they're published and you're not.)
- Do not ignore their advice!

Next to commentary from an editor, a critique from a published, professional author is something worth paying for. But it's given out for free! All the time!

You might be thinking, "No one does that stuff. No one sends dead cats or even writes scathing e-mails." Well, you're wrong. As a literary agency reader in Los Angeles I received angry e-mails from authors I had rejected, but I have a better story. One of the authors I contacted about reading one of my recent books, Douglas Preston (*Relic, The Codex, Tyrannosaur Canyon*) declined to read my book.

Was it because he was a mean guy? Not at all. He'd recently received several death threats from different authors to whom he'd given advice and not written a blurb for. Thus, he no longer reads books and writes blurbs. So, writers do retaliate angrily and they end up eliminating the possibility for the rest of us to have our books read. What you should do is thank them for the wonderful advice, promise to buy their next book and ask if it might be possible to send them another book in the future. They'll probably say yes.

On a side note, I met Douglas Preston this past November and was able to give him *The Didymus Contingency* as a gift of appreciation (*The Relic* was the book that inspired me to become a writer so many years ago.) I'm out $10 for the book, but my odds of getting a review from Douglas Preston in the future went up a notch that day. Even if you get rejected by an author, be nice. It can pay off.

5

MARKETING PART 1

All right. Now we're getting somewhere. You've passed your own personal scrutinizing, you've had at least one decent editor comb your work for typos, clichés and plain old bad writing, you've received a good blurb from at least one author (which is now gracing the front and back covers of your book) and you have some advance reviews in the pipeline. The cover is primo and the interior layout is equal to, nay, better than traditionally published books. Now it's time to sit back, suck on a stogie and watch your Amazon sales rank drop lower than the temperature in Antarctica.

Hmm, time for a reality check.

1. Amazon sales ranks only go down to 1. The temperature in Antarctica drops well below that, so scratch that analogy from your mind's hard drive.

2. Smoking, stogies or otherwise, is nasty! What were you thinking?!

3. Books don't sell themselves. As a POD publisher this is your job.

And it's a very hard job. I'll look at every aspect of marketing a book that I have used, all of which have contributed to my book's success. Remember, I am probably just like you, a poor starving artist, and the good news here is that I didn't spend a dime on marketing. OK, that's a lie. I spend a few dollars a year for my web hosting plan. But that's it!

WORD OF MOUTH

This is a natural phenomenon that occurs when any one human being experiences something they enjoy. When you see a really good movie, what do you do? You tell people. If you go skydiving and found it thrilling, you'll probably tell all your friends and attempt to have them come for your next jump. The point is, when people really like something, they want to share it with the world...they want to spread the joy. It's human nature.

Word of mouth is the force to which I attribute a vast amount of my sales. I received several e-mails saying something like, "so and so recommended your book to me and...add glowing comments." But this past summer, I witnessed the true power of word of mouth sales first hand. I was having a book signing at a

Waldenbooks. The day was winding down and the majority of people had come and gone. Then a woman showed up with her husband...and bought seven books, one for each of her children, who live all over the country. Apparently she had been in the store previously and *The Didymus Contingency* was recommended to her by a guy named Frank Ferris (my first true fan and now friend). She bought the book, loved it and then brought it to be signed with plans of having seven more signed for her family. That one person sent the book to seven more and if they like it as much, the potential sales from that single recommendation are astounding.

So how can you the author, tucked away in an office, unseen by the public do anything to kick start the word of mouth domino effect?

Step 1. Write a good book! Seriously, there isn't much more you can do to help yourself than to take my advice from the beginning of this book and be honest with yourself. If your book is solid and undeniably good, word of mouth will occur naturally.

Step 2. Encourage everyone who lets you know they loved the book to extol the book's virtues to everyone who crosses their path. I get several fan letters a week and you better believe I ask each and every one of them to spread the word. Many let me know they already have, but some who may have kept their opinions to themselves are more than happy to help out, especially when I let them know the book has no marketing dollars promoting it. Finding a good book that needs promotion is like finding a cause worth fighting for. People love to root for the underdog...and as a POD author, underdog is beyond understatement.

BOOK SIGNINGS

This should go without saying. If you publish a book, you need to set up some book signings. But as a POD person, your ability to do so is somewhat limited. First of all, you don't have a publisher supporting your campaign, so big signings in New York City and Los Angeles are probably out of the picture (unless you happen to live there). Second, bookstores generally don't carry POD books... WARNING! I'm about to get sidetracked for a paragraph (or two).

It's true. Bookstores do not typically stock POD books. This is one of the larger detractors from POD publishing. However, this does not mean it is impossible. Barnes&Noble is particularly open to consignment sales. This means that they take a percentage of every sale, typically 40%. My local B&N was nice and only took 20%. This is a good deal because if you were a small press and used a distributor to get your book in stores you'd lose about 60% per book (though you'd be in many more bookstores). I'm just saying the percentage is fair.

For those who don't know how consignment works, here's the breakdown. You buy the books at whatever author discount you receive. You set the sale price (I chose to sell mine for $16 in store—the suggested retail price is $18). You drop the books off

at the bookstore, they put them on the shelf, and hopefully someone buys a copy. At the end of every month (or quarter) the bookstore should cut you a check for the sale of the book minus their
percentage. Consignment at Barnes&Noble is a formal process in-
volving a few pages of paperwork, but they're great at being
prompt with payments and that paperwork helps keep track of
how many books were delivered and how many sold. Smaller
stores might not require paperwork, but you might also have to
bug them for payment. Either way, consignment is the primary way
to get your book stocked in brick and mortar bookstores.

Of course there are exceptions to this rule, which I discovered
for myself. Borders and Waldenbooks (now the same company)
have very strict regulations for book signings. I approached my
local Waldenbooks and asked, "I had this book published, might it
be possible to have a book signing?" The manager kind of laughed
and then handed me Borders' list of qualifications I had to meet to
schedule a signing. The list included:

Must guarantee at least 26 sales.

Must provide own advertising.

Must print own full size, full color posters.

The list went on and on, but basically said, "You cannot have a
book signing unless you're famous." I read to the bottom, which
sealed the deal in my mind.

Book must not be a self-published or print-on-demand.

A flurry of expletives and rants about corporate America flashed through my mind, but instead I said, "Well, how about I show you the book anyway?"

The manager humored me. I handed her the book. She read the back copy, eyebrows rising. "Hey," she said, "This sounds pretty interesting." Then she glanced up to the top of the page and read the blurb from James Rollins.

She gasped. "My assistant manager loves James Rollins!" She pointed to the shelf where two copies of each of Rollins' books were being sold. I knew my chances of having a book signing improved when she got a sneaky look in her eyes. I immediately told her to "keep the book, give it to your assistant manager and call me if something can be worked out". See how handy author blurbs can be? They open doors traditionally closed to POD authors.

They called a few days later and scheduled a covert book signing (we were breaking all of Borders' rules). The signing went off without a hitch, the turnout was great and Waldenbooks ordered 45 copies of my book...directly from Ingrams (the wholesale company for my book), not on consignment. All that is to say, consignment is the rule...but some managers do bend the rules.

That was way more than two paragraphs.

While walking into a bookstore and handing the sales person a book is one way to go, and it did work for me, I wouldn't recommend it. I know better now. Here is what you will need. A press kit.

What's a press kit? It's basically a folder containing any positive reviews you've received, articles about the book, interviews you've done and a copy of the book...for them to keep. You can also include promotional material like bookmarks or posters, but I think that's over-kill. I was advised by a friend of mine (A Customer Relations Manager (CRM) at Barnes&Noble) that all that really matters in a press kit is the book itself. You can have the greatest promo material in the world, but if the book stinks, they're not going to invite you to have a signing.

So now you're angry at me because a press kit costs money. They're about $12 each including the cost of the book, prints and whatever promotional materials you decide to make. However, I also said that I didn't use them. I should have. I was lucky that the quality of my book was good enough (and the blurb from Rollins impressive enough) that getting signings wasn't too hard. I also had a history with the local bookstores. I'd done signings for my first, traditionally published book, *The Screenplay Workbook*, previously, and had run several free workshops in the stores. It's always good to keep up positive relationships with the folks who schedule signings!

For great information on putting together a press kit and to see photos of a very professional press kit, laboriously type in this link:

http://www.lulu.com/forums/viewtopic.php?t=25974&highlight=stacey+cochran

Here, fellow Lulu author, Stacey Cochran, has put together a wonderful message board post on creating a press kit. I imagine he spent more than $12 per kit, but I also imagine they came in very handy.

So, press kit in hand, here's what to do next. Remember the CRM I mentioned? That's who you need to speak to. Most Barnes&Nobles have a CRM and they are the person who schedules book signings, Christmas gift wrapping events, writers' groups and anything that involves someone having an event in the store. Always call your B&N before going in. You want to meet the CRM face to face. If the CRM is not there, do not simply leave your book and press kit. Every time I have done that I have not received a response. There is no connection there. It's easy for them to say no. CRMs get inundated with authors requesting signings so whatever you can do to make a connection, do it. I have never been turned down for a signing when I met the CRM in person.

On that note, when you go in to meet a CRM, do dress nicely. Don't wear the clothes you might put on for a day of writing. Wear something that says, "I'm a professional author." Even though your book is a POD consignment title they're going to know you mean business.

You might now be wondering why book signings are important. There are several reasons.

1. They expose you and your book to the book buying public (it's a bookstore after all).

2. They are FREE marketing. Book signings don't cost a dime (other than your fancy shmancy press kit).

3. Book signings allow you to meet readers and make personal connections with them. This is important because if a reader has met you and likes you, you better believe they're going to tell all their friends and family about you and your book. Meeting an author gives many people a thrill and bragging rights. I think it's hysterical when I meet someone at a signing who heard about me somewhere. They act nervous; like *I'm* someone famous. I know better, but to them I'm someone important. As a new author, this is very fun and uplifting, and can keep you pushing your book when it seems like sales will never pick up.

Make sure to schedule book signings for the first few months after your book is released. As more and more positive reviews come out, your chances of getting non-local signings increase. Slowly work your way out from your area. Who knows, you might make it to New York after all!

WEBSITE

There are few cheaper or more effective ways to market you and your book than a website. A website is available for the entire world to see and can contain as much information as you need to sell your book. On my website, www.jeremyrobinsononline.com I have information on both of my books (including reviews, samples and cover images). I offer a shopping cart via Paypal so readers can buy signed copies directly from me for the same price they'd pay on Amazon. There is also a blog (updated at least once a week to keep those interested informed about my writing), a FAQ for those seeking publishing advice, a picture of my mug, a bio, and an appearances and signings page for those looking to meet me and get a signed book in person. The point of all this is that potential readers will come away knowing more about the books, about me and about how to buy a book. It's about marketing, but it's also about making that elusive connection with people. It's about making yourself friendly and available. Once that connection is established people are more apt to not only buy your current books, but also to check out your next.

But maintaining a website, especially a good website, is not easy.

First you need a host. This is a business that holds your website files and makes them available to the rest of the world. I personally recommend godaddy.com. They're very large, very affordable and had their commercial banned from the SuperBowl. Okay, that's not really a credential, but maybe you now remember them.

Before you rush out to godaddy.com and register your domain name, first consider this. Can you put together or have someone put together for you, a decent website? If you can't, perhaps put it off. Just like the book cover, image says everything. If you have a poorly designed website, those who find it might be quickly turned off by your frilly pink fonts on yellow backgrounds, your over-use of free GIF animations and your dead web links. Sound like any websites you've been to? You know the ones. You leave without reading a word. If this is the best you can pull off, save your money for something else.

If you have Microsoft Office and know how to use Word fairly well, there is hope. Some versions of Office come with software titled FrontPage. This is basically a website designer that works exactly like Word. If you know how to insert images and manipulate text within Word, you will most likely be able to put together a decent website in FrontPage. My entire website was designed with FrontPage. There are also numerous books on how to use Front-Page and other website software, or if you're ambitious, write the html code from scratch (I don't recommend this). Rather than try to turn this into a website tutorial, I'll make this suggestion: to save money, search on Amazon for the books you think will help the most and then request them at your library. That's what libraries are there for!

The one hint I will give about websites is this. Make sure you include META tags. What are META tags? It's basic information (keywords and description) about your website that search engines access when scouring the web for search results. This is how Google and many other popular web search engines find websites, by searching for keywords within the META tags and within the text of the site itself. This increases the chances of your website popping up in a search engine. Any good tutorial or web design book will tell you how to add them in whatever software you end up using. Many web hosts, godaddy.com included, offer free website design software. It's typically pretty basic stuff, but it might get the job done. If Office is too pricey to buy (and I know it is) this might be something worth looking into when you're searching for a web host.

Don't underestimate the power of a website. I receive several e-mails every day from my website. They've come from those considering buying my book, fans who have read it and loved it, my current agent and several international publishers, many of whom have since purchased the rights in various languages. This is your portal to the world. Make sure it's clean, professional and available and it will work for you, day and night, all around the world.

BLOGS

This is actually something new for me. For the first few months, my website had a message board. This was fine. A few people posted messages, but it really kind of just sat there. I think they're great for established authors whose fans really enjoy communicating with each other, but as a new author, many people don't know what to talk about. There isn't much history and they have no idea what's coming next. So I switched to a blog. I now post updates on my writing between 1 and 3 times a week. At first I was sure it would fade into obscurity just like the message board had, but it hasn't. People are reading it regularly now and I often get e-mails from other authors starting out who read it to feel inspired or get encouragement. I never thought my random notes on writing (or not writing) would be interesting to anyone but me, but it's turning out otherwise.

How this helps me, in many ways more than the rest of the website, is that readers of the blog are along for the ride. They read about every challenge, every success and every defeat. They cheer you on. They back you up. They buy your next book. Why? Because they know you. You are now not just a mysterious writer who seems to come up with great story ideas. You're a human being who struggles to develop a story and who picks himself up after being rejected. You become someone worth supporting. There are few better ways for an author to connect with fans. On average I have more hits to my blog than to my website, so I'm now reaching twice the amount of people than I was with my website alone. Blog readers can also leave comments, making each blog a message board as well and reinforcing the idea that message boards are fairly useless...for me anyway.

As for the who, what and where. I use *www.blogger.com*. It's free and there is a large community of people who use it. I instantly had people viewing my blog and I did nothing to advertise it. Blogs also appear in Google and since they're updated frequently, often get higher listings in the search engine. Having never used a blog before, I found blogger.com perfectly easy to use and understand.

I've never had a technical issue with them and highly recommend their service to anyone desiring a closer connection with fans and potential fans.

E-MAIL

This might seem like an odd subject to have in the marketing section, but I assure you it is not. E-mail is essentially your way to communicate privately with everyone involved with your writing career. Whether they be fans, publishers, agents, editors, readers or inquiring minds, this is how you will most likely speak with the majority of people you do business with.

That said, there are a few rules you need to abide by as a professional author. I'll make this simple. When you write a letter do you punctuate? Of course. Do you capitalize? You'd better. Do you use bright colors and funky fonts? I hope not. Do you finish your letter with "Sincerely," or something like that? If you're nice you do.

Basically, you want your e-mails to be formatted like a professional letter until a relationship is established. Be professional in everything you do. The only real difference between an e-mail and a letter is that in an e-mail you don't need to indent new paragraphs. For some reason it looks funny and is generally acceptable not to indent when you add a line between paragraphs...though no one will care if you do either. Otherwise, keep your e-mails looking sharp.

So you think that's it, do you? All done with this e-mail bit, right? Not by a long shot. We still have two more points to cover and if you haven't thought of one of them you need to go cut a branch from the backyard, fashion a switch from it and give yourself a good, old fashioned fanny tanning.

MAILING LIST

A mailing list is a list of e-mail addresses to which you will regularly send updates about your book. Every time your book gets a good review, send it out. Every time sales peak to some kind of best-selling status, send it out. Every time you're doing a signing or workshop, send it out! You get the idea. This is a group of people that are frequently updated about your book. Of course, make sure not to send your updates too often or people are more likely to get annoyed. I would say once a month is the max, and only that if you actually have interesting news to share.

Start the list with people you know...everyone you know. Family, friends, distant relatives, co-workers, ex-co-workers. Everyone. Make sure to include a sentence, something akin to, "If you want to be removed from this list, please let me know." If you don't include that little bit some people will consider the e-mail SPAM. I started with a list of about 60 people I knew. Everyone who sends me an e-mail about *The Didymus Contingency* gets added to the list. It's now a very long list and not one person has asked to be re-

moved. That means this very large group is being constantly re-
minded about my book. And when they hear good news about my
book, they're able to stay excited about it.

What this leads to is word-of-mouth. If your book is on people's minds they'll talk about it. The people they talk to will talk
about it and so on. The more people you get talking and keep talking about your book the better. A e-mailing list is the perfect way
to secure a group of loyal fans who don't have to get online or find
your blog to stay informed.

PUNCTUALITY

What does being punctual have to do with marketing? When you're
responding to an e-mail, responding fast says volumes. It says,
"Your questions and interest are important to me," and they
should be. I respond to every e-mail, preferably the same day I receive it or the next day. If I don't, I apologize for not responding
sooner. The response I get 100% of the time is extreme gratitude
and excitement.

When you send an e-mail it is sent instantaneously to the recipi-
ent. Chances are, the person you've sent an e-mail to received and
read it right away. You know this. Everyone knows this. If you go
a week without hearing back from someone you've e-mailed it's
generally safe to assume that your e-mail wasn't important enough
to garner a response.

The psychology of a quick response helps an author out immensely. It builds that bond between you and your fan, colleague or critic. It makes you reachable and not so scary. Remember, to fans of your book you are an author just like any other. The way you might feel about sending Anne Rice an e-mail (nervous, timid, silly) is how some people might feel about emailing you. I can think of several authors I've written to and received instant replies from. It's a wonderful feeling to know that an author thought your e-mail was important enough to respond to right away. I can tell you I will continue buying those authors' books. I can also remember a few authors who never replied to my e-mails. I still think they're fine authors, but I'm hardly as excited about their books as I used to be. You can bet I'll pick up the books by the nicer, more open authors first.

Be the nice author. People love nice authors. And being prompt makes people's day. It's really not that hard and you'll make a lot of long term fans that way. Remember, the way you present yourself is as important as the way you present your book. People tend to judge a book by its cover, but they're likely to judge it by its author as well.

PRESS RELEASES

A press release is the standard way of letting the media know about you and your book. For best results you need to have a hook that makes your release interesting. I know you think that having your book published is newsworthy (though it might be in your home town), but it's probably not, especially if it's self-published.

For a release being sent to local papers, try to combine the information about your book with news about a book signing, workshop or public reading. This will increase your chances of getting in the paper.

If there is any controversial aspect to your book capitalize on it. Make sure your press release mentions it. Basically, you need to find some other reason you and your book are newsworthy aside from publication. Here is the press release I sent to my local papers via e-mail, to the news editors.

FOR RELEASE ON *DATE HERE*

Jeremy Robinson

ADDRESS HERE

PHONE NUMBER HERE

info@jeremyrobinsononline.com

CONTROVERSIAL NOVEL PUBLISHED

May 01, 2005 – "The Didymus Contingency", (Trade paperback, 289 pages - $18.00) an eyebrow raising novel, written by local author, Jeremy Robinson, has been released worldwide by Lulu Press. It is available through Barnes and Noble, Borders, Waldenbooks and at online booksellers such as Amazon.com.

The story is premised on a single question, "If you could go back in time and witness any event, where would you go?"

The answer for the book's main character, Dr. Tom Greenbaum, an embittered atheist and quantum physicist, is: the death and failed resurrection of Jesus Christ, a goal which he vigorously pursues throughout the story.

A hair-raising adventure ensues as Dr. David Goodman, Tom's colleague and closest friend follows Tom into the past, attempting to avert the time-space catastrophe that would be caused by proving Jesus to be a fraud. But forces beyond their control toss them into a dangerous end game where they are tempted by evil characters, betrayed by friends, pursued by an assassin from the future and haunted by a demon that cannot be killed.

James Rollins, international bestselling author of Ice Hunt and Sandstorm claims, "Jeremy Robinson's novel, *The Didymus Contingency*, blends the cutting-edge science of Crichton with the religious mystery of the Left Behind series to create his own unique and bold thriller. It's a fast paced page turner like no other. Not to be missed!"

"It's my hope that everyone can enjoy this novel," says Robinson. "My intent is to tell a story surrounding the life of Jesus without sterilizing it. Most people react positively to the book, but some have a problem with the harsh language and violence, not to mention the fact that many Biblical characters, including Jesus, appear in several scenes not actually recorded in the Bible."

"It certainly isn't my intention to rewrite the Biblical record of Jesus," says Robinson. "This is a work of fiction, after all, and should be read as such."

Editors: Author photo and book cover images are available upon request. The author is also available for interviews and appearances. Contact Robinson using the above contact information.

Finding that controversial element resulted in a front page article with a full color photo. What a thrill it was to be recognized around town and the book signing a few weeks later was packed. Locally, a good press release can work wonders.

However, nationally or internationally, press releases are much harder to make useful. You can send out free press releases at *www.prweb.com*, but I have found them to be fairly useless. I'm sure people read them, and that is good and makes them worth my trouble, but don't expect the press to come beating down your door. Thousands of press releases go out everyday and let's face it; the publication of a POD book isn't exactly news. Even during my bestseller days my national press releases and one put out by Lulu.com failed to gain any attention. You might still choose to send out a release, and you might get lucky and be noticed by the media, but don't set your hopes high. It's more likely that your release will fail to gain any attention. If your time is limited I would recommend putting your efforts into something that will garner tangible results.

AWARDS

A great way to get your book noticed and legitimized is to enter, and place in well known contests. Suddenly your book is not just a book, it's an award winning book. You're no longer just an author, you're an award winning author. Even if you're a finalist and not the grand prize winner, it still says a lot for your book. Of course, if you enter and lose...keep it to yourself.

Believe it or not, there are several contests specifically for self-published, POD or small press books. The literary world is starting to take note of the books being self-published. The fact that an author has taken the time to put a book together says they're serious, but pile accolades on top of that determination and people see an author who's determined *and* talented. In many ways, the contests serve as a proving grounds. Many publishers and agents keep track of the results because the contest does a lot of the work for them, weeding through the many books submitted to find the few really great reads.

Here are the biggest and best of the competitions. If you can place in one or more, you would be off to a good start. But be warned, this can be a painful way to discover your book is not as good as you think it is. That, in itself, can be a valuable lesson. Many of the competitions also provide you with ratings materials which reveal how your book failed in the eyes of the judges. What you learn from these rejections can help you improve so that if you ever take a chance with a second book, you'll be better prepared.

FOREWORD MAGAZINE

Not only is Foreword magazine one of the most important places you need to have your book reviewed prior to publications, it also offers a great contest for small presses and self-publishers (including PODs). Their opinion is very well respected and many libraries, agents and publishers pay attention to the reviews and contest winners.

Foreword magazine offers 60 contest categories (increasing your chances of winning) and two grand prizes in fiction and non-fiction for $1500 each. While there are no monetary prizes for winning your category, the award is prize enough. There is an entry fee of $60 that is well worth the price. For more information visit:

www.forewordmagazine/awards

THE INDEPENDENT PUBLISHER AWARDS

Otherwise known as the IPPYs, this contest is very similar to Foreword's contest. There are 60 categories, again increasing your odds of winning. There are ten overall top spots, each receiving $500 and then there are winners in each individual category. When all is said and done, if you're a winner, you can order stickers announcing your book's award for placement on your book's cover that (in theory) help sell more books. But the real prize is recognition. The entry fee is $65.

Be warned: entering this contest will put you on a mailing list for Jenkins Group. They're the company putting on the contest, but they're also in the business of book marketing, so you'll be hit up for their services every now and again. For more information visit:

www.independentpublisher.com/ipaward.lasso

WRITER'S DIGEST SELF-PUBLISHED COMPETITION

By far the hardest to win of all the contests, because of the lack of categories (9), and the sheer number of entrants, is the Writer's Digest competition for self-published books. If you really want to test your metal, this is the place. The entry fee is $100. The nine grand prize winners "receive $1000 cash and promotion in *Writer's Digest*. In addition, Book Marketing Works, LLC will provide a guaranteed review in Midwest Book Review and a copy of Fern Reiss's book *The Publishing Game: Bestseller in 30 Days.*"

"Plus, all Grand Prize and First Place winners will receive book-jacket seals to promote the award-winning status of their book, promotion on the *Writer's Digest* web site at writersdigest.com, a copy of *The Complete Guide to Self-Publishing, 4th Edition* by Tom and

Marilyn Ross, $100 worth of Writer's Digest Books and a Notable Award Certificate."— from the Writer's Digest website.

As you can see, this contest is so appealing because you get much more than money and the ability to claim an award winning status. You also get help promoting the book after the fact. This is a great contest to win, but the competition is fierce. For more information, visit:

www.writersdigest.com/contests/self_published.asp

WORDS OF WARNING
KEEPING YOUR COOL

Being available via a website, blog or e-mail opens you up to both fans and critics. And the majority of the time critics are the most vocal. You might receive praise from ten true fans, but one critic can undo all of the encouragement you've received.

Critics tend to assault rather than critique. They make personal jabs and often exaggerate and verbally gesticulate like they have to convince the world that your book is the worst thing in existence.

Our natural instinct is to fight back, even more so than when we get a rejection from an editor or a harsh critique from another author. After all, it's just some half-wit spouting off, right? You're a writer. You can take him in a mental chess match. Perhaps so, but that's not the point. This is someone who already feels angry at you. For some reason your writing was not what they expected. The story wasn't what they thought. Whatever. The point is that they're irate and ready to tell the world.

That's what you don't want them to do. One bad review on Amazon can kill five good reviews. If you respond angrily, you better believe the person on the other end (who has nothing to lose) is going to start a campaign against you. They can easily post bad reviews, knock you on message boards, dedicate a website to your demise and tell everyone they know that you're a joke. Negative word-of-mouth can hurt you as much as positive word-of-mouth can help.

What you should do is respond kindly. Even apologize for letting them down. I recently received my one and only scathing e-mail from a gentleman in Ireland who loathed my book enough to write and tell why. He went so far as to say he blamed me for taking away a few hours of his life that he could not reclaim. My response was, "Thanks for writing. Sorry my book wasn't right for you. Your critique inspires me to continue improving as a writer." Only it was three paragraphs long and much better written.

I could tell he wanted a fight. He was on the edge of doing his best to demonize my book. But my response defused the situation and probably made my critic loathe me a little less. Who knows, maybe he'll even come around some day.

As a developing author you're going to get attacked. It's inevitable, but it really does help to turn the other cheek...unless the critic shows up at your front door with a 2x4. Then you should just run like heck.

6

MARKETING PART 2: AMAZON.COM

As a POD author/publisher, brick and mortar bookstores are for the most part off limits. This means that the majority of sales are going to come via the internet. Your book will sell at Barnes&Noble.com, Buy.com, target.com, booksamillion.com and many others. But the sales from every other online retailer combined won't touch the number of sales you get from Amazon.com. They are the number one online retailer and seller of books. This is no accident. Amazon, more than any other online retailer, is set up so that shoppers can easily communicate to each other what products are worth buying and which should be ignored. This includes your book. There are programs Amazon offers, and they're always adding more.

I have noticed, especially lately, that Amazon is trying out new programs fairly regularly. This means that exciting new programs might only last a few weeks. For example: about three months ago (that would be October, 2005) I discovered something new on my Amazon page for *The Didymus Contingency*. It was a form that allowed Amazon members to write technical information about topics covered in the book. I thought it was a great idea, and people were actually using it. The concept behind it was essentially the same as Wikipedia.com (an online, editable encyclopedia). But two weeks into the program it disappeared, never to be seen again.

*Upon finishing the first draft of this book, this service has returned. It is called a Product Wiki. It might be worth giving it a try, but I'm not going to discuss it in detail because it may again disappear.

I've noticed a few other programs come and go, so rather than focus on every program Amazon is offering at this moment, I will focus on the ones that have stood the test of time. This will hopefully keep confusion to a minimum, will stop any, "hey, you said..." e-mails, and will allow you to focus on programs that won't disappear after all your hard work.

All of this is public knowledge so forgive me if it's not news to you. When I started out a year ago, the inner workings of Amazon were totally unknown to me, but thanks to author David Rising, who guided me through the Amazon process during my first month of publication, I came to realize Amazon held several tools for the POD publisher to use.

TAGS

Amazon describes these as, "Think of a tag as a keyword or category label. Tags can both help you find items on the Amazon site as well as provide an easy way for you to "remember" and classify items for later recall."

What we're focusing on is the, "help you find items on the Amazon site," portion, because the tags not only help *you* find items on Amazon, they help *everyone* find items Amazon. And if you set up the right tags, people might just find you.

Here's how tags work.

On the Amazon page where your book is listed you'll find an area labeled, "Tag this product." You simply apply a word or phrase that labels the book appropriately. "Great Book," "Thriller," "Gift4John," all work fine. It's a brief description of the product or the reason you want to remember it. This tag creates a link back to your profile using your screen name, where all of your other tags are listed. And you need to have other tags listed for this to work at all. It also creates a tag to a list of other books other users have tagged the same. So if you click on a "Good Book" tag, you're going to be taken to a list of other products people have tagged "Good Book." Your book would now be among those listed.

Here's a play by play of how the process would work. Let's say I've tagged my book and twenty others. For the example we'll say I've tagged them all as "Thrillers". Among those books is *The Codex*, by Douglas Preston (a great book). Now, everyone who views *The Codex* page on Amazon is going to see my tag. There is a chance that some of those people will click on my tag to see what other thrillers I've tagged. People are always on the lookout for new books and new authors. Checking out what other people have tagged might lead them to a new gem. When a person clicks on my screen name tag they're taken to my profile where it shows my list of tags, including the other "Thrillers"...which, of course, includes my book. If my list of thrillers is populated by other well known authors, chances are that my name is the only one they won't know and will take a look. The other option is if they click on the "Thrillers" tag itself. They'll then be taken to a much larger list of books labeled "Thrillers" by other Amazon members. Your book might be harder to find here, but at least it's listed.

Essentially, you're adding your book to a database under the listings you want. It's not the easiest way to get noticed, but the tags make your book more visible than with no tags at all. Something most people don't understand is that even though your book is listed on Amazon, the chances of being found unless someone knows the title of your book or is searching for your name, are very remote. You can have an amazing book, but if no one knows it exists, no one can buy it. Tags are one of the ways you can make your book visible on Amazon.

The last bit of information you need to know about tags is that in order for them to be viewable to the public they have to be created by an account that has actually bought something on Amazon. So don't bother creating a few tags if you haven't actually bought anything from Amazon; you'll just be wasting your time.

LISTMANIA

This has become a popular method for POD authors and even small presses to get their books noticed on Amazon. According to Amazon, Listmania lists are, "a list that includes products you find interesting. Lists can have up to 25 items. Your lists will appear on Your Profile page and other places at Amazon.com."

First I'll explain how to make a list and then describe how it will help you. To make a list simply visit a book page, product page, a search result or your profile. You'll find a link labeled, "Create Listmania List." Click on this link to open the Listmania page. First you'll want to label your list. Something like, "Romance Novels of 2006" is appropriate (if your novel is a romance). After this, there is a field for entering your qualifications for making the list. This can really be anything, but you could write something like, "Author," or "Romance Reader."

Now it's time for the list itself. One by one you need to add ISBNs of other books you want in the list. For this fictitious list we'd be adding romance novels, preferably ones that are selling like hotcakes. The reason for this is because your list will show up on the product page and in searches where the books in your list appear. As an unknown author, your romance novel wouldn't normally turn up in a search for "Romance" and it still won't. But if one of the other books in your list shows up, there is a chance your list will as well. If it does, the list will appear on the right side of the screen. If you've been bold enough to put your book in the #1 spot, there is a chance your book cover will even show up! This means your tiny little book has a chance to show up at the top of search. This is free marketing that can't be beat.

Be warned that some people believe it is rude to put your own book at the #1 spot and reveals that it was, in fact, you who created the list, but I'm not one of them. Free marketing is free marketing. Take what you can get. Your cover image showing up in a search result is like having your book on display in a bookstore. People will notice it.

Once you have entered the ISBNs in your list you have the option to make comments about each book. As the author of your book I would recommend not writing something like, "The rest of the books in this list stink in comparison to my #1 book." You might really believe that, but unless you're revealing yourself as the author of the book, it's not honest. You should either leave the comments blank or give unbiased descriptive summaries about each book. At the same time, I would recommend encouraging friends to create lists as well. They can say whatever glowing comments they want about your book.

The one thing you don't want to do is flood the system. Avoid making identical lists over and over to increase exposure. What you'll end up doing is having the same list appear three times. This is bad because people will be annoyed that there is no variety in the lists, and it will also hurt everyone else creating lists. The lists only work if people are using them, and people will only use them so long as they remain useful. Over-populating the system with list clones will create disinterest in the long run, and then we'll all be out of luck...and sales.

Listmania lists are one of the best ways to make your book visible on Amazon, placing your cover image in search results and on the product page for similar books. There are few better free advertising opportunities available online (that I have found.)

SO YOU'D LIKE TO...GUIDES

This is a program on Amazon that is in some ways similar to the Listmania lists, though more detailed. They're basically articles written about a genre, subject or group of books. Three books are featured at the top of the page and a longer list of all books mentioned is listed at the bottom of the page. Of course to get the

most attention for your book, it should be one of the three featured books, but don't force it. If it doesn't make sense to have
your book in the top three, don't put it there.

Here's an example. If your book was science fiction, you could
do something like, "Discover something new in Science Fiction."
So the whole thing would read, "So You'd Like To...Discover
Something New in Science Fiction." Then you'd list your sci-fi
book with two others. Provide detailed descriptions of all three
without going overboard about how great your book is compared
to the others. As with the Listmania lists, have your friends create
some So You'd Like To…s or let your mailing list know that they
exist. *They* can gloat about your book as much as they want to, and
that works for you!

To create a So You'd Like To... simply visit any Amazon product page, search result or your profile. Each will contain a link labeled, "Create A So You'd Like To...Guide." Click the link and
follow the instructions on the page. The process for creating a
guide is more complicated than a Listmania list, but can be less
time consuming. On Amazon, these guides rank second behind
Listmania lists for advertising potential. They're viewed far less often, but contain more details about your book. If you can provide
good information about your book and the others in the guide, it
should bring people to your book on a regular basis.

REVIEWS

Herein lies one of the biggest selling points on Amazon and one of the most tempting pitfalls for an author. Good reviews on Amazon can and will sell your book. Many people, me included, are apt to buy a product that has nothing but glowing reviews. To utilize this you must get people to write reviews! I accomplished this by reminding everyone on my mailing list a few times to write a review if they liked the book. My efforts resulted in a few good reviews. The other way I keep good reviews coming is through fans. This seems obvious, but many fans who write to me haven't posted reviews. I thank them for their compliments and then mention the idea of writing a review. Most have and it helps a great deal. All of the Listmania lists in the world can't help you if the majority of customer reviews you get are bad.

The temptation here, of course, is to post several reviews yourself. Not only is this dishonest, but you'll probably be found out. Not right away of course, but when people start buying and reading your book, they might notice that the book is not nearly as good as the reviews claimed it was. You'll quickly find your online book listings covered in angry, scorn filled, negative reviews. Some people might even go so far as to claim the author must have written his own reviews...and they'd be right!

Of course reviews like this are also due to people having different taste in what they read. I recently received a negative review from a reader who bought *The Didymus Contingency* based solely on the book's glowing reviews (when in fact, not all are glowing) but he felt lied to by the positive reviewers and claimed that they must have all been written by my friends and family...which was not true. Here's what he said, "Don't believe the blazing 5 star Amazon reviews. They only prove that the writer's real talent is the abundance of family members and distant relatives, willing to offer a positive review." The end result of this review will be a dip in sales until another fan or two posts a good review, but at least I don't have myself to blame. It's kind of nice to have so many good reviews that people think they must be fake!

If friends who have read your book post a review (which is fine) urge them to be honest. Ask them to temper their reviews and if they noted something wrong in the book, mention it. Positive yet informative reviews will not result in backlash as much as glowing, seemingly exaggerated reviews.

The point is, people are watching. Some people have nothing better to do than to investigate new authors and make accusations. But I don't believe they're totally out of line, because many authors do place multiple reviews of their own book. It might help your sales initially, but if you're found out, you can kiss your reputation good-bye.

REVIEWS PART 2

Another technique people use on Amazon (and other online bookstores like Barnes&Noble.com) is to write reviews of other books and promote their own book at the end of the review. This isn't necessarily inherently evil, but it can be used inappropriately.

If you're going to review another book simply to add a promotional line for your book at the end, at the very least, read the book you're reviewing! It's incredibly obvious when a review is vague and then at the end gives a glowing review for another book. It only makes you and your book look foolish. People are not easily tricked. Read the book before you review it. If your review is honest and helpful, people will value your opinion and your recommendations. If you post a fake review, your book will be avoided. I promise.

As usual, I have a story to illustrate my point. Like Amazon, Lulu.com members can post reviews. Over the past months I have received about ten reviews on Lulu, nine positive, one negative for *The Didymus Contingency*. But what I noticed about all of them was that they all referred to or recommended other Lulu authors' books. As the author of the book being reviewed, Lulu offers me the option to make reviews available only to people who have actually bought the book. I activated this option for *The Didymus Contingency* and guess what...every single review disappeared. I had ten reviews from people who hadn't even bought the book! If only I could do this at Amazon, I have a feeling some of those reviews (good and bad) would disappear as well.

Beyond posting a review for a book you've never read, it's also not appropriate to write a review of your book within the review of another book. I've seen authors include blurbs for their own books that are almost as long as the "review" they're writing. What you should do is something more like this: at the end of your real review, write, "Also recommended: Your Book by Your Name Here." But don't stop there! Add other books that you've enjoyed as well!

Why would you list other books? They might go to those books and not yours! This is true, but there is a good reason. As a reviewer your goal is to help the people reading your review. By giving them a better selection you're letting them know you have good taste. By seeing the other books you're recommending, they know you have the same taste in books as they do. If they look at any one of the books you recommend, chances are they'll look at all the books.

I'm sure this works sometimes, but it is probably one of the more ineffective techniques on Amazon. I'd advise reserving it for when you're actually writing a review. Don't go out of your way to write twenty reviews in one day. It's probably a waste of time and people will notice that you wrote twenty reviews in one day that all recommend the same book. You might think no one will notice, but trust me, someone will.

SEARCH INSIDE

This is one of the most well known programs at Amazon. A book that has Search Inside enabled can be searched through by keywords. It allows Amazon members (who have purchased something) to read portions of your book and get an idea for the quality and writing style. It also allows page visitors, member or not, to read the first chapter of your book.

This is great for people whose books are professional. Your writing can sell the book better than any review. But for those books that aren't quite up to snuff, this can hurt your sales. I'm not saying, "If your book isn't that great, hide it from readers." That's silly because you'll just end up with bad reviews and your sales will tank regardless. What I am saying is almost becoming a redundancy in this book; if your book isn't ready, isn't professional, don't publish it!

Another benefit to Search Inside is that it makes every single word and phrase inside the pages of your book searchable through a product search. This makes your book more visible to those using the search option.

Here's how Search Inside works. After signing an agreement, you send Amazon a copy of your book. They'll slice and dice it into individual pages and scan each and every one into the system. The text pages are converted into a searchable database and the front and back covers are displayed. *FYI- they don't always do the best scanning job. To see what I mean, visit my book, *The Didymus Contingency*, on Amazon and click on the Search Inside option. I don't think they even attempted to scan my cover straight.

To send your book to Amazon, simply visit any book page (including your own) and scroll down to Product Details. At the very bottom, under sales ranks, you'll find a link, "Publishers and Authors: Improve Your Sales." Follow this link. On the next page are three options. The middle option is Search Inside. Follow the "Learn More" link. Here you will find a brief description of the program, but what you want is the "sign up" link in the lower right. From here you need to fill out the sign-up form and then wait for a confirmation e-mail from Amazon. After this, you mail in your book and wait about three to four months for your Search Inside option to show up. It really does take a long time to go through, but can help sustain sales once it appears.

Some other fun options available through Search Inside are SIPs (Statistically Improbably Phrases), Citations (if you reference other books in yours, they'll be listed here), Text Stats (which reveals readability, complexity, word count, sentence count and other fun things like "words per dollar") and a concordance (shows the 100 most used words). It's all very interesting and very cool. It serves to reveal information about your book. If you've got a great book, this can only help.

PRODUCT UPDATES

When you publish a POD book, your POD service should handle listing your book with all of the online retailers. How this is done varies between POD services, but the end result is the same. Your book will be listed on Amazon and the original book description you wrote will show up too.

But your job is not done! Depending on the online store, you may need to upload a cover image. Most websites add your cover image automatically, but some do not. If that's the case, you need to e-mail the cover image to each individual site. Every web retailer is different and has varying requirements. Instructions for most can be found in the help section of the individual websites.

But the primary website you should really concern yourself with is Amazon. Remember, this is where the majority of your sales will originate. Here's how to upload cover images to Amazon. Please note that these requirements and procedures may change in the future.

First, the image needs to be in the correct format.

- TIFF or JPEG format.
- 72 dots per inch resolution preferred
- A minimum of 500 pixels on the longest side

- sRGB color mode

- 8 bits per channel

- PC or Macintosh format

- File names must consist of the 10-digit ISBN (no dashes needed), e.g., "6004435678.tif" or "1254545332.jpg"

- Image should be a full front view of the cover, with no borders

After that, you need to send an e-mail to *image-fix@amazon.com*. They will give you a user name and password that you'll need to send them your cover image via ftp. If you need ftp software, I recommend Ace FTP 3, which is freeware and can be downloaded at: *freeware.aceftp.com*. Instructions on how to use whatever FTP software you decide to utilize should be available in the software's help file or on the software's website.

You should also constantly update your descriptive text, adding blurbs and reviews, rewording the summary for effectiveness, etc. To add descriptive text to Amazon you must go to their publisher update page. Rather than list out each of the five or six links you need to follow to find this page, I'll simply give you the obnoxiously long web address.

http://www.amazon.com/exec/obidos/tg/browse/-/13685601/ref=br_bx_c_1_0/102-9594993-6917769

Once you're there, do yourself a favor and bookmark the page. If you are pioneering and want to find the page for yourself (which I did) just go to the Amazon Help page and start at the Publisher

& Vendor Guides link. Once you're at the publisher update page, you will have to type in your publisher information and the ISBN for the book you're updating. The publisher information for each POD will be different. As a Lulu.com publisher, I put in Lulu's information.

After this you will be brought to a long form where you can add information about your book, about the author and much more. I recommend adding enough to make people interested but not so much that it's overwhelming. Make sure everything is written as clearly and concisely as possible. This is your official area, as author and publisher, to make your case for why a customer would want to buy your book. Like everything else you do, this needs to be professional. People know these blurbs are from the publisher and if they smack of amateurism, your book's value will be called into question. I'd suggest observing how other books in your genre are presented on Amazon. Do your best to mimic the marketing style and material and you should be all set.

CATEGORY LISTINGS

When your book is first listed on Amazon, chances are your book will be added to a generic category. You want your book to be listed in as many categories as possible. You can't force Amazon to add your book to categories, but you can suggest them. I suggested about ten categories and they gave me three. I did the same at Barnes&Noble.com and they gave me five. Both are fair and both increase my book's visibility within those specific categories.

To update your categories on Amazon I would start by visiting the pages of books similar to yours. Look at their category listings, pick those you feel are appropriate for your book and copy them for later. Once you have a list of ten categories, send an e-mail to Amazon at: *book-typos@amazon.com* and to Barnes&Noble.com at: *bookcorrections@bn.com* or *databaseerrors@bn.com*.

The subject line should include your ISBN and the purpose for writing. You should also make sure to repeat the ISBN in the e-mail itself, along with the book title and who you are. Here's the e-mail I sent to both Amazon and B&N:

My name is Jeremy Robinson, author of *The Didymus Contingency*, ISBN:1411627148. I was hoping you could update the categories the book is listed in (it presently isn't listed in any). I have done a thorough search and have come up with the ten best matches, which I've pasted below. Thank you for taking the time to update the page. I appreciate it greatly.

Sincerely,

Jeremy Robinson

This was followed by a list of ten categories. Here's what one of the ten looked like.

Fiction & Literature: Fiction, Thrillers, Christian Thrillers

Because I was listed in these categories I am now able to say that I've been the #1 Christian Thriller and the #1 Action Thriller on Barnes&Noble.com. This increased my visibility exponentially. Many people look at the bestseller lists and I'm happy to be placed in many of them on B&N and Amazon (though that changes all the time).

Updating your categories should be done right away. It is a permanent change and will make your book available to people searching those specific categories, especially if your book is selling well...which is the point of all this!

INTERNATIONAL AMAZON

In addition to the main U.S. Amazon site, Amazon has sites in Japan, Germany, Canada, France and the U.K. While the sales from these site are not as high as the U.S. sales, they are important. I've sold about 40% of my books to overseas customers. In fact, my overseas sales eclipsed my domestic sales in January, 2006. They are a viable and important market, especially to the small publisher.

While the other Amazon sites don't offer the wide range of options that Amazon.com does, they all offer Listmania lists, which is enough. *The Didymus Contingency* has been an Amazon Canada bestseller three times and is generally ranked between 1000 and 3000. At the time of writing this, I am ranked 1,246 overall but am also the #2 Religious Mystery behind *The Da Vinci Code*, the #2 Biblical

Fiction behind *The Red Tent* (a long time bestseller) and #5 in Action/Adventure, a much broader and more competitive category.

Obviously, in these categories I am highly visible and that can only help. Also, hitting a #1 spot in these categories (which I have in all of them) allows me to use those numbers as marketing tools. "POD author, Jeremy Robinson replaces the Da Vinci Code as the #1 Bestselling Religious Fiction at Amazon Canada," sounds pretty good.

In addition to making sales overseas, you also increase your chances of being noticed by foreign publishers. I've been contacted by many large, overseas publishers interested in *The Didymus Contingency* after seeing it online. I now have several translation deals with publishers because my book is listed on foreign Amazon sites.

If time is limited I would suggest focusing your effort on Amazon Canada and Amazon U.K. While I've had sales in France, Germany and Japan (highest rank was 500), they remain significantly lower because of the language barrier.

Take advantage of the international Amazon sites and you should find your sales dramatically increased.

The web addresses for all the Amazon sites are:

Amazon U.S. – www.amazon.com

Amazon Canada – www.amazon.ca

Amazon U.K. - www.amazon.co.uk

Amazon France - www.amazon.fr

Amazon Germany - www.amazon.de

Amazon Japan - www.amazon.co.jp

In closing, as a POD author/publisher you are going to sell 95% of your books online and probably 90% of these at Amazon. And it just so happens that Amazon is perfectly set up for free advertising opportunities. If you pass on utilizing the Amazon programs, you are giving up sales.

WORD OF WARNING

HONESTY

What has become the central theme of this little book is something you need to consider in depth as an author. Why is honesty so important? I could preach about morality and right and wrong, but you should already have a grasp of these concepts. Unless you believe morality is subjective; that it's not wrong to steal a few dollars from a millionaire because he'll never miss it. So the morality argument is either obvious or falling on deaf ears. Why then, does honesty benefit you, the author?

The answer is reputation. If you lie, you're eventually going to get caught. You see it in the news all the time. Reporters creating stories. CEO's cooking the books. Celebrities... being celebrities. If you get caught in a lie, you'll eventually be exposed. You will be embarrassed. You will be undone. Few things kill a career faster than an untrustworthy reputation.

Consider this possibility. You create a bunch of fake reviews for your own book. Everything goes great for a while and your fake reviews result in a slew of sales. Good news right? Your next royalty check is in the high hundreds. You're making progress. Now all those people who read your reviews and bought your book are posting reviews of their own. It turns out your book isn't as great as you claimed. Why isn't it good? Because you weren't honest with yourself about how prepared you and your book were to be published. So now your readers are let down. They're angry for being ripped off. They're suspicious. Then someone says it, "The author must have written all these reviews!" Once that's on the page, everyone else who comes along will run with it until, to the viewing public, it's the truth and you're a liar.

Two years later, having been discouraged by your POD nightmare on account of your dishonesty for some time, you decide to take another swing at POD. You put your book out and this time around the reviews are real...and they're great. You've done it for real this time. Then, unknown to you, an agent sees your book and is interested. But this is a smart agent and he does some research. He quickly finds your first book and reads the account of your false reviews and the angry slew of readers it resulted in.

Now the agent has something new to consider. Your past practices as a writer are called into question and your reputation may have been damaged enough to hurt future sales. Taking you on is now a risk because your reputation reflects on his. In the end, the agent decides you're too much of a risk and passes you by without you even knowing. It'd be a shame, wouldn't it? I know this is an extreme example, but it happens. People lose entire careers all the time because they took the easy, dishonest route in the beginning. It may be more painful, but try your best to stay honest. In the long run (and there is no short run in the writing world) your honesty will pay off.

7

DESIGN HINTS AND TIPS

COVER DESIGN

As I've mentioned, you need to have an A+ cover. It needs to be, in every way, indistinguishable from a traditionally published book.

A great cover conveys several messages to people all at once. A good cover communicates the style and content of the story. I can generally tell if I'll like a book or not by its cover because a lot of thought went into the design and how best to promote the story. An ambiguous cover tells nothing about the story and potential readers will move on to something that catches their eye. Beyond that, a quality cover says, "The publisher really believes in the potential of this book." How does it do that? Not all traditionally published books get great covers. It's true. Some are just plain awful and that is because the publisher didn't feel the potential of the book was enough to put more time and money into the book's cover. If it's not going to sell boatloads of books regardless, why put extra effort into a snazzy cover? Whether its conscious or subconscious, people know this is true and shy from books with ugly or boring covers, traditionally published or not.

The last and most stigma busting element of a good cover is that people will not assume your book is self-published! You can do nothing better for your book than to make it appear as traditionally published as possible. As a writer I tend to look at the publisher of every book I read, just to see who's publishing what. But most people never look at the publisher if it looks like a quality book. The exception to this rule is if the book looks self-published. Then, many people check for a publisher and if they find it's self-published, quickly move on. A good cover is the first step to *not* giving someone a reason to think your book is self-published. \

I highly recommend getting a professional to do a cover for you, but fully realize not everyone can afford such a thing. If I were not an illustrator/graphic designer, I'd be up the creek with the majority of other POD people.

My first recommendation is not to create your cover in Microsoft Word or some other word processor. Nothing shouts, "avoid me," more than Word Art for a title. I apologize to any readers who've done this. I'm just being honest. What you will need, if you go it alone, is photo editing software. Chances are, if you own a scanner you have some kind of photo editing software, but most bundled photo editors don't have the teeth to put together a quality cover.

The best photo editor is Adobe Photoshop, but unless you're loaded, this is not going to work. And if you're loaded, hire someone to design your cover! If you do manage to get Photoshop, be aware that many of the cooler effects come from Photoshop plug-in programs, such as Eye Candy 4000, and these need to be bought separately. A cheaper alternative to Photoshop is Paint Shop Pro. This software generally sells for $60. But even $60 can be a lot for the starving artist. So I've put together a list of free photo editors that you can download.

GIMP - *gimp-win.sourceforge.net* – This is often referred to as the "free Photoshop," and is supposed to be capable of most Photoshop functions.

Serif - *www.freeserifsoftware.com* – Serif offers a slew of design packages for free including PagePlus SE (desktop publishing tool), PhotoPlus 6.0 (a photo editor), WebPlus 6.0 (for web design) and several more creative options.

Pixia - *park18.wakwak.com/~pixia* – Originally developed in Japan, this one has been modified into an English language version that appears to have all the tools necessary for laying out a cover image.

PhotoFiltre - *photofiltre.free.fr* - A French developed photo editor that is light on options, but easier to use.

DESIGN TIPS

• **Keep it simple**. Multiple images, loud fonts and bright colors quickly turn people off. Try to make it exciting without going overboard.

• **Add some red.** Might sound silly, but it's one of the first things you learn in design school. Find a way to add a dash of red and people's eyes will be drawn to the cover.

• **Use modified photos.** The background image on my book is a photo I took at Joshua Tree National Park in California with a lousy 1.2 megapixel digital camera. It's been run through a watercolor filter to give it a stylized look. It was simple, and it works effectively.

• **Your name in lights**. Logic says that because you're a new author you should make your name tiny on the cover. That's what big publishers do with new authors, right? Sometimes, but consider this. Most people assume an author's name is large on a book cover because he's popular or bestselling. They assume the author is established. Take advantage of that assumption! Make your name large enough to imply you're not a nobody. It will help people believe your book might be worth buying...after all, your name alone must be enough to sell books. Why else would the publisher make it so large?

• **A good title goes a long way.** One of the most important aspects of your cover is the book title. Make sure it's easy to read and eye catching and dissimilar from other books.

• **Blurbs.** You don't want to cover your...cover... in quotes, but a brief snippet will catch people's attention. It will let them know that someone has approved of the book and chances are that they'll look at the back for more. Just make sure there are more!

• **Fonts.** This is important. The font you choose needs to be readable, but it also needs to convey the style and genre of your book. Using something boring like Times New Roman or an illegible script is going to give you away as a POD person. There are plenty of free fonts available online, find one that best suits your story. I recommend *www.fontfreak.com*.

WORDS OF WARNING
COVER NO-NOS

1. When designing a cover it is tempting to pull images off the internet and use them as your own. This can land you in serious trouble if the owner of the image notices. However, you can modify images so that they're something totally different. I'm not talking about something as simple as color change here; the end product has to be something completely new, something no longer discernable as the original (as people do with collage). That is acceptable. But never use an unaltered image taken from the internet without permission. And this should probably be your last resort.

2. Do not make up blurbs! Yes, people do this. Just because your uncle Lou works as a janitor for the NY Times, you cannot give a blurb from him and say it was from the NY Times. You should also avoid creating fictitious magazines, newspapers or authors. This is a silly practice and is an easy charade to uncover. If you're having trouble getting blurbs or positive reviews, reread the chapter on being honest with yourself.

3. Some POD services provide ready-made covers. You can just type in your title and name and whamo, you've got a cover. No, no, no! Do not do this! The cover designs are usually not the greatest, but there are even better reasons to avoid them! First, ready-made covers convey nothing about your story. How can a potential customer know anything about your book if the cover is some random image? Second, the text that gets slapped on the cover is flat and boring and fonts are limited. Third, hundreds, perhaps thousands of other POD books being published at your POD service will have the exact same cover! You need to separate yourself from the POD stigma, not put on the uniform and stand in line. Stand out from the crowd.

INTERIOR LAYOUT

For me, this was a grueling procedure. It took about a week of research to learn everything I needed to know. If you're using Word I'd recommend buying a how-to book, or preparing to hunker down and do some research to get it right. What's worse is that there is no magic formula for laying out a book's interior. Each book is different. Each design requires different skills. Once you know what your design should look like, then start figuring out how to get that done. It may be a long frustrating road, but don't stop until you're totally satisfied.

Avoid using templates because they're generic and not formatted for your genre. Every genre has its own interior style. Chapter fonts and illustrations vary from book to book. Make sure your book fits its genre. For example, if your book is a Western, you wouldn't want to use a Star Trek font for chapter headings. You also wouldn't want to use a standard font like Ariel either. You'd want to use a font that smacks of the story you're telling and is appropriate for the story the cover represents.

For the actual prose in your book I recommend something standard and simple like Garamond, which is the font I used for this book.

Your book needs to be seen as a total package. Cover, interior design and story need to mesh seamlessly. The best way you can make sure you're on the right track is to look at the interior design of other books in your genre. When I laid out *The Didymus Contingency* I had a stack of about 20 books on my desk from authors like James Rollins, Douglas Preston, Lincoln Child, Matthew Reilly, Jack DuBrul and Clive Cussler. I took the most common elements in all of them and made sure my book fit the look. Learn from the traditionally published books. The more you can mimic their design, the harder your book will be to distinguish from them. And that, in the end, will help you immensely.

8

FAQ

The following are actual excerpts from e-mails I have received about POD or about Lulu.com and my actual answers. They may be redundant at times, but they should give you a good idea about some of the things most people inquire about.

Q: I was just wondering if you'd mind telling me a bit about your Lulu experience? How is the book quality, waiting times etc. I also noticed that on Amazon, your book says "usually ships within 24 hours" and "this book ships from amazon.com". I thought that normally POD books had a different message and an extra fee on Amazon? Is this because you sell books directly to them or did Lulu set something up due to you being a best-seller?

A: Lulu has been great. Book quality is excellent. Everything has moved at the proclaimed speeds and the one time I had a problem with a shipment (the books were warped) they replaced them the next day. The only warning I ever give people about Lulu is that you really have to be a do-it-yourself kind of person. Lulu does such a good job that if a book fails it has nothing to do with Lulu and everything to do with the author. Make sure you can put together a good looking (covers and interior) and well written book. Many Lulu authors don't. Last, make sure you have some kind of marketing plan. Many authors think that if they throw together a book with an ok cover and slap it on Lulu that people will see it and buy it. Not so. So with Lulu, they hold up to their end of the bargain, but most authors have no idea what they're getting into (myself included...I just happen to have a fairly quick learning curve and an unnatural amount of determination).

As for Amazon... I think many Lulu books list as 24 hours, etc...if they're selling. Sometimes my timeframe drops to 8-12 days or something around there, but within a day or two it's back to 24 hours. From what I understand, if a book is selling well Amazon will actually stock a few in their warehouse. So when one sells, it goes out from the warehouse and they order a replacement. As for the cost...the books that sell via Amazon, B&N, etc. do have a higher cost. Mine has a suggested retail price of $18.00 on these sites. On Lulu it sells for $15. So it is more expensive. Most POD books of my page length do sell for more, but I decided to lower my royalty to keep sales down. My goal was to sell a lot of books, not get rich.

Q: Did you do your cover and book design through Lulu?

A: I did the book cover and interior design myself. I have a background in illustration and graphic design so it worked out well for me. Lulu doesn't offer cover/interior design, though they do give links to folks to do. I can't vouch for those services. Hiring someone is your best bet if you don't have any graphic savvy friends.

Q: How can I check sales through Ingrams?

A: Ingrams has an automated phone service you can call. The number is 615-213-6803...and that was from memory...I never use it...right. When you call that number it will ask for your ISBN so have it handy. Type in the number, hit 1 to confirm and then chose option #2 to hear the current week and the previous week's sales. Keep in mind that sales do come from other places. Foreign sales printed in the UK (for example) don't show up in this database. I've also noticed that actual sales tend to be higher than what Ingrams reports via this number. It is a useful tool to see if the book is moving though...and it can be addicting.

Q: Now that you have an agent will you even use POD again?

A: It would be nice if I didn't have to, but I'm not opposed to it. My other novels are all very different from one another and the chances of my agent liking them all is doubtful. I see no reason not to publish books through POD that my agent might pass on. I enjoy the process.

*This is obviously true now that I'm publishing POD People via POD. I discussed it with my agent and we agreed that it would be hypocritical to pursue a traditional publisher with this book. It only made sense to publish it through POD.

Q: Do you read POD books and provide blurbs?

A: This is something I have recently begun doing. I will read books that are similar in genre to my own. Don't bother asking me to read romance or literary fiction. I probably won't like it, even if it's good for those genres. I've read and provided blurbs for some great books like *Golem* by Greg Vilk and *The Seventh Mountain* by Gene Curtis (which is one of the best books I've read this year).

I'm not sure how far my opinion will help your book, but it's better than nothing!

Q: Have you ever bought a printed POD book?

A: Honestly, no. I've read a couple good ones (that were sent to me for free) but I believe the bad stigma surrounding POD books is well deserved. I've read so many that made me cringe. This doesn't mean I never will, but I have yet to see a book put together good enough to catch my attention. I can tell you this. If I ever purchase a POD book, chances are I won't even realize it's POD, because the author will have done his job.

Q: Do you create covers for other authors?

A: I've dabbled with the idea of creating covers (for a price) but it's not something I plan on doing full time. If I really like a story or concept I might offer, but it's generally something I won't do (mainly because being paid to create art takes the fun out of it for me.) One cover design I did that I like is for *The Magician* by Crystal Hickerson.

Q: I was hoping you'd be a new champion for print-on-demand self-publishing. I'm disappointed to see that you've removed all evidence that the book was published through Lulu. Why did you do that? You shouldn't be ashamed of being a POD author.

*Lulu places a logo on the spine and their website address on the back cover unless you opt to have them removed, which I did.

A: Lulu is great and I have no shame in being a Lulu author, but to openly promote your book as self-published or POD is just plain bad marketing. I'm not a famous author who decided to self-publish and be a champion to the cause. I want to sell books...for me. I want to be an author for a living, meaning I won't always be publishing through POD. Books that even lightly smack of self-publishing are typically avoided. I'll be a champion of that...of making POD books indistinguishable from traditional books. That's something I can get behind. That's the only way POD authors and publishers can really benefit.

Q: As a POD author, where is the best place to get my book reviewed?

A: There are several important reviewers to consider (like Midwest Book Review) but for a reviewer that focuses solely on POD books there is only one place to go: POD-dy GIRL, located online at: girlondemand.blogspot.com. This traditionally published author (whose identity is a mystery) writes one review a week (approximately) of only POD books. The odds of actually getting reviewed are slim, but if your book is good, nay great, the odds are on your side. I know for a fact that agents and publishers watch this blog (mine does) so getting reviewed here is a great thing all around. She also has a yearly contest (the Needles) in which she picks the best of the previous year's books and has some agents and publishers judge which are the best in literary fiction and in commercial fiction.

WORD OF WARNING

SCAMS

There are few things more damaging to your career and to the POD community as a whole than scams. By this I mean that authors of POD books find ways to boost their sales without anyone actually buying their book. Its sounds outrageous, but it happens, and this past summer I witnessed it myself.

In August of 2005 *The Didymus Contingency* was moving quickly up the sales ranks at Lulu.com. I believe I was ranked around 18 at the time. I had recently moved into the spot of bestselling fiction on Lulu and was feeling very proud of that small victory. Then, out of the blue, two books zipped ahead of me. I will keep the book titles and author names to myself. This was surprising because both books weren't even in the top 100 previously. They seemed to come out of nowhere.

Strangely enough I was soon contacted by the two authors with a request at doing a group press release. It seemed like a good chance for promotion and I agreed. What I would soon discover is that these authors were trying to legitimize their own books by linking them with mine. Why? Because their sales were gained through illegal means. How is this possible?

Both authors placed orders with Barnes&Noble. Not the website, but the physical stores. These weren't small orders mind you. They were hundreds of books, possibly thousands! The books were printed up and marked as sales, but when they arrived at the store for pick-up, no one came for them. B&N quickly caught on, removed the book from their website and notified Lulu, who also pulled the books. The authors were busted.

This all happened just before the scheduled press release was due to go out, which was great for me because it never went out and my reputation was never sullied by being linked with the scamming authors'. I do not know the fate of the two authors, but I imagine it was expensive. These kinds of actions do nothing to further your career and make booksellers even more wary of POD books. For the sake of POD People everywhere, avoid scams!

9

INTERVIEWS

This chapter consists of three interviews I have done. They further serve to answer any questions I have yet to cover or forgotten to cover in the book thus far. Some of the questions may be similar between the interviews but my answers vary and reveal details yet to be disclosed.

INTERVIEW WITH JEREMY ROBINSON, HIGHLY SUCCESSFUL LULU AUTHOR

October 17, 2005

by Parker Owens

posted on *www.blogcritics.org*

Did you try to publish the traditional way before embracing self-publishing? Can you talk a little about your experience and frustrations?

My venture in traditional publishing has had both ups and downs, but *The Didymus Contingency* was never sent to or rejected by a traditional publisher. My first book, *The Screenplay Workbook*, was published in 2003 by Lone Eagle Publishing. This was a great success and the book is still doing wonderfully and used as screenwriting curriculum at many schools.

But non-fiction and fiction are two different beasts. *The Didymus Contingency* was my first novel. I'd been writing screenplays for years (12 screenplays at the time) and decided to go on hiatus from screenwriting and write a novel. When I was finished, the manuscript was put on the shelf. I continued writing screenplays, thinking the novel bug was out of my system. I was wrong.

I wrote my second novel, *Raising the Past*, a year later (2003) and have completed two more, one in 2004 and one in 2005. I have been shopping *Raising the Past* around, with little luck. Partly because I'm very picky. I sent the manuscript to two publishers and maybe five agencies. So I know the frustration of rejection, but not on the grand scale many authors experience. And now that I have an agent, that has been to my benefit. The field is still wide open for him to play in.

Ultimately, I chose self-publishing for *The Didymus Contingency* because its content and style (a Christian thriller written for a mass market audience – it contains cursing, drunkenness, graphic violence...) would make finding a traditional publisher as an unpublished novelist very tricky. James Rollins, author of *Map of Bones,* and *Sandstorm,* also advised me it might be the best route for the book (for which he provided a blurb – as seen on the cover.)

Can you tell us a little about the Christian market, and if you were trying to sell your book to that market?

As I mentioned, it is a Christian book in the sense that it involves Jesus in a positive way, but the way I chose to write it (and the way I choose to write in general) was for a mass market audience. I didn't censor myself or my characters because I might offend other Christians. I don't see how an author can truly portray the real world while censoring what characters do and say.

That said, I have only heard good things from Christians who have read it and all have found the cursing, drinking and violence to be in good taste and necessary to the story.

What made you choose Lulu to self-publish the book?

I was extremely skeptical about self-publishing when I began. I am well aware of the stigma placed on self-published books, and without a ton of money to spend on marketing, I knew I was in for an uphill battle. When I started searching for self-publishers online, it was really just for fun. I saw many that cost a bundle up front, from hundreds to thousands. I found several that were less expensive, but didn't offer global distribution or ISBN's. And some required you to use their custom made covers. After spending an hour here and there over two or three days, I came across Lulu.

Lulu sold me on self publishing. The only money I had to spend was on the copies I ordered and the global distribution package, which I believe was around $150 at the time. My total cost was under $200, including three beta prints so I could make some revisions and style changes. That is something just not possible anywhere else that I know of. The best thing is, I made my money back in the first month after the book's release.

In addition to Lulu's fantastic pricing was the fact that I could design the interior and exterior myself. This was music to my ears. Before writing, I was an illustrator and graphic designer. Being a bit of a control freak made Lulu the perfect fit for me. Before it was released, I could tweak the book until I was 100% satisfied...and it didn't cost a dime.

Does Lulu offer editorial services, and did you take advantage of them?

I cannot say for certain if Lulu offers any official in house editing services (though I don't think so), but I know they allow others to post their services on the website. I didn't use any services because my wife is an excellent editor and my professional editor from *The Screenplay Workbook* edited *The Didymus Contingency* for free.

Do all Lulu titles have an ISBN, and are they all listed on amazon.com and b&n.com?

You have to pay for the ISBN. There are two packages: Basic Distribution gives you an ISBN and adds your book to Books in Print. It makes your book accessible to bookstores, but not available online (though it would be online at Lulu). This costs about $35.

I chose to go with Global Distribution. This adds your book to Books in Print, but also enters you into Ingrams' (a major distributor) database. Your book becomes available on Amazon (in the U.S., but also in Canada, Germany, the U.K., France and Japan), Barnes&Noble.com, Borders.com and just about every other online bookseller in the world including places like Target, buy.com and Wal-Mart.

By comparison, the closest service to Lulu I was able to find was IUniverse. The cheapest package there with global distribution was $460. Granted, they format the interior of the book, but that's nothing a little elbow grease can't take care of. But the single biggest reason I chose Lulu over IUniverse, and the reason I'd advise avoiding IUniverse is this. You have to sign a (3 year) contract, giving IUniverse the worldwide English license to the book! You can cancel the license, but it takes 30 days to go through. That makes them the publisher, not the author, and it takes away a ton of control.

Lulu is a far more customizable service and is much more affordable. That said, I am envious of IUniverse's Star Program, for which I would qualify...

How many copies have you sold?

I'd like to keep numbers to myself, but I can tell you this. Most print-on-demand books are considered a success if they sell 500 copies total. I passed that number in the first two months, which was much quicker than I anticipated.

Do you attribute any of your book's success to the similarity with Da Vinci code?

Not at all. It has been compared to Da Vinci a few times but it really shouldn't be. This is happening to just about every religious thriller published today. Any story that involves Jesus or the Catholic Church is now a Da Vinci rip off. I'm a Dan Brown fan too, but he didn't invent the genre. For those in disbelief, check out The Da Vinci Legacy, published in the 80's. Dan Brown is following in the footsteps of those who paved the religious thriller road, just like me.

The only similarity between *The Didymus Contingency* and *The Da Vinci Code* is that they include some aspect of Jesus in the storyline and both titles start with 'The D...". The similarities end there.

Many people have written and said they enjoyed *The Didymus Contingency* more than *The Da Vinci Code* and I'll accept that, but when I hear comparisons, it just reveals the person commenting has only read the back cover.

Can you tell us a little of your marketing plan?

My marketing plan was sheer genius! No, wait...I didn't really have one. I put together a mailing list of about 200 people and inundated them with release dates, cover images and the like and annoyed them into forwarding the information to everyone they knew, and so on. A lot of the initial sales I would attribute to that effort.

The sustained sales are coming primarily through word of mouth. Most people that buy the book recommend it to others. One woman bought seven copies at a signing, one for every member of her family...and no, it wasn't my mother. Other than that, I have the website and several good reviews from official book reviewers like Round Table Reviews and Christian Book Previews.

My plan was to make the absolute best book I could and let it sell itself. So far, that's working.

To what do you attribute your incredible success?

When the book hit the Barnes&Noble.com bestseller list, I was in shock. That it hung out there for a few days and took the #1 spot in Christian Thrillers and Action Thrillers surprised me even more. It has also been a best seller on Amazon Canada several times over now. The primary force behind the success of the book is the book itself. People really enjoy it and the word is spreading. I'd also like to think, that being a Christian novel, perhaps I've had a little divine intervention on the book's behalf!

Have you done any book signings? (And how did you make that happen with POD?)

I have had two book signings so far, one at Barnes & Noble, the other at Waldenbooks. Both were extremely successful, with books being sold out. At Barnes & Noble, I had done signings in the past for *The Screenplay Workbook* (three, in fact) so I had established a relationship there and getting in again was just a matter of asking. However, with Barnes & Noble I had to bring my own copies to sell on consignment. Because they are print-on-demand, they are not returnable and thus, B&N will not stock them (though they kept three consignment copies for the shelf).

For Waldenbooks I simply went to the store and asked, 'Do you sell self-published books?" to which they replied, 'No, we are run by Borders now, and here are their rules." I read the rules and was pretty much guaranteed that A. I'd never get my book in the store, and B. I'd never schedule a signing. Regardless, I took out a copy and offered to let them keep and read it. The manager looked at the cover, read the blurb from James Rollins and everything changed in that instant. 'Oh! My assistant manager is a huge James Rollins fan!"

The assistant manager took the book home, read it, and loved it. I had the first book signing at this Waldenbooks in two years scheduled within a few days. The book is now stocked in the store at all times (ordered through Ingrams, *not* through me on consignment) and is right up there on the shelf next to who else? James Rollins.

Tell us how you were discovered by a mainstream agent.

I was sitting down for a day of writing and like every day I began by checking my e-mail. 'Receiving 1 of 1..." flashed across the screen. Then I saw who it was from: a literary agency whose name I instantly recognized. I thought, 'Why are they writing to me? Did I submit something to them?"

As it turned out they had seen *The Didymus Contingency* on Amazon, did some research on me, read the good reviews and decided I might be worth their while. They weren't even aware of the book's B&N bestseller status, which it had achieved the day before. They asked for a copy of the book, which I sent out immediately, and within a few days, I had an offer for representation. I gladly accepted.

My new agent has just begun shopping it around domestically, but there has been an offer for the Romanian rights (for a Romanian translation) and interest from a large German publisher (for a German translation) as well.

So far, the book, and Lulu have far exceeded my expectations. My plan was to sell 10,000 copies and then approach publishers and agents. Now, thanks to rising interest in the book and the exposure offered by Lulu, I don't have to worry selling 10,000 copies. So far it's been every self-publisher's dream come true.

When do you anticipate hitting the 10k mark?

Honestly, I don't anticipate hitting it at all. I hope my agent sells the book to a traditional publisher. I decided not to put too much effort into a continuing marketing campaign, because that will be important when the book is republished. If the book doesn't sell for some reason, I will set a new 10k goal and ramp up marketing efforts, but right now my eyes aren't even on that prize. Instead I'm focusing on my fifth novel, something closer to the genre of *The Didymus Contingency*, to follow up on the book's eventual (hopeful) sale. At the current rate of sales, without any marketing on my part, it would take about three years to hit the 10k mark.

INTERVIEW FOR WWW.DOUGSMITH.INFO

Tell us about yourself and your background and your writing life.

Let's see…My background is actually in art. My college major was visual art and my goal was to be a comic book illustrator. I was on my way to a career in comics having done a few covers for independent books, a one shot issue of my creation, *Ralph,* and then getting a job as both illustrator and writer for an indie comic company. But my excitement for the industry waned as the comic book industry entered the dark ages of the 1990's. Most comics being published at the time were more about cleavage and thongs than actual story telling. This was punctuated by the announcement of my new publisher that they would also be publishing pornography. I immediately jumped ship.

Ultimately I discovered that getting paid as an artist was a hard thing to do. Finding work was easy. Receiving a check in the mail…not so easy. I decided to keep art as a hobby (which I still do) and move on to writing for another visual medium—film.

I began writing screenplays while my wife and I traveled the country for four months in a beat up station wagon, in which we hauled bedding, clothes and a full sized computer. We traveled up and down the East coast. It was during this time that I wrote my first, and most pitiful screenplay. Thankfully, I wrote several more over the years and eventually, when I thought I was ready, moved to Los Angeles to pursue the career in earnest. Things moved quickly in LA. I had an internship at an agency in two weeks. I landed an agent in six months. Some of my work was optioned, even in development (actually, it was the screenplay version of my currently published novel that was in development). Towards the end of my stay in Los Angeles I wrote and sold my first published book, *The Screenplay Workbook*, which is still doing well today.

While in LA I wrote *The Didymus Contingency*, based on my screenplay titled, *Didymus*. That was the beginning of the end for my screenwriting career. Having had our fill of the Hollywood lifestyle we headed back to the East coast and clean air. Now I'm writing novels nonstop (five so far) and I'm not looking back.

What is your daily writing schedule?

I attempt to write every day from 1pm to 5pm. My wife and I take care of a man with disabilities and have a 16 month old daughter so some days don't permit the full four hour time span, but it's my goal. If I'm reaching the end of a book I'll usually write at night as well. I tend to write a chapter or two a day, which can be anywhere between 5 and 15 pages. My top page count in one day was 25.

What are some of your favorite books, movies and music?

Favorite books include just about everything by James Rollins, Michael Crichton, Douglas Preston, Lincoln Child and most recently,

Steve Alton. I'm kind of a science based action/adventure junky and that's what I tend to write. Absolute favorites would be Deep Fathom by Rollins, Prey by Crichton, MEG by Alton and The Relic by Preston/Child.

As for movies, I'm two flicks short of a complete Godzilla collection, but ultimately Aliens by James Cameron stands as one of my favorites. But my biggest influences from the silver screen are Spielberg's Jaws and Close Encounters. Though lately I've been on a kung-fu kick with Crouching Tiger, House of Flying Daggers and Hero.

Music is a tough one. I listen to just about everything except country and boy bands. While writing I listen to soundtracks. Favorites are Time Machine, Pirates of the Caribbean and War of the Worlds. I suppose some of my current favorites for music are: Korn, U2, James Brown and Tenacious D…I did say I like a variety, right?

How would you describe yourself as a writer (genre, vision, etc.)?

I tend to find a bit of science fiction in everything, but the genre I've found myself in is Thriller. Whether I'm writing about aliens, mythological monsters, demons, time travel, space travel or some Arctic adventure eventually someone's going to be running for their life.

However I do write for two very different audiences. First is religious thrillers. This would include *The Didymus Contingency*. I have three novels for this genre. While the action and writing style is unaltered from my other works, the storyline revolves around some aspect of the Christian faith. My other two books, and hopefully my sixth, are more main stream thrillers similar to Crichton, Rollins and Preston. They may or may not have moral messages in them, but they have nothing to do with the Christian faith.

Did you already have an agent or did publishing on Lulu enable you to get looked at by an agent?

I had an agent for screenwriting in Los Angeles. Shortly after returning to the East Coast I had to let her go because she did not want to work on the novels (but still expected a royalty if something sold.) When I came to Lulu and published *The Didymus Contingency* I did not have an agent.

It was solely because I chose to publish with Lulu that I found an agent, or I should say, that an agent found me. It is because of my book's visibility on Amazon that an agent discovered my book, researched me on the internet and sent me an e-mail. Six weeks after publishing with Lulu I had an agent at one of the most reputable agencies in NYC.

Why the switch from a screenplay to a best-selling book?

The switch was for three reasons.

1. I was tired of Hollywood. Being from New England I like straightforward answers and honesty. Hollywood is the exact opposite.

2. After writing *The Didymus Contingency* I found novel writing much more rewarding. I could add details and plot twists I had to leave out of screenplays because of page limit and production costs. And while the publishing world may not be nicer than Hollywood...they are, at least, more honest.

3. With novel writing only one other person touches the story—an editor. Any changes are made by me personally. A publisher doesn't hire eleven other authors to come in and fix (kill) the story like they do in Hollywood. The story isn't further modified by directors, actors and producers. This is why most authors don't like the film versions of their novels. The movie that's made rarely reflects what is actually in the novel.

You warned that POD authors will need to use 'elbow grease.' Can you elaborate on that? What are the pros and cons of publishing like this?

The amount of elbow grease ultimately depends on where you publish and how well you want your book to sell. There are plenty of POD outfits that do a lot of the work for you, but you'll be replacing elbow grease with cash. For me, I went with Lulu, who is the cheapest POD option available. I did the cover, the interior layout and the typesetting. That visual art background came in handy. But as a POD author you also have to do all the marketing, all the planning, the budgets, the public relations, etc. You are not just the author, you are the publisher. It's a two fold job. Granted, first time authors at traditional publishers have to do the majority of promotion for their book, but at least they don't also have to design, stock and edit the work.

What does the public think of POD? How about bookstores and libraries?

The public doesn't know much more about POD than that it is a method of self publishing...and that, they don't like. There is a stigma around self-publishing that kills most books before they're available. Many POD books on Amazon have scathing reviews simply because they're self-published. My general advice for people considering POD is to make the book as identical in quality, both visually and written, to books that are traditionally published. Most people do judge a book by its cover.

Unfortunately, the public's opinion is not entirely unfounded. A good percentage of POD books are printed by people who have been rejected for whatever reason by traditional publishers. Many of these books do need to be rewritten, edited better and are often not professionally designed. But there are some people who decided against the traditional route from the beginning. I decided my chances for finding a publisher for a book like *The Didymus Contingency*, a religious (Christian) thriller written with a mainstream approach, would be better if I produced it myself. So far, that's proving true.

Even with the large number of bad POD books, this is my general opinion: Do we only buy paintings that were commissioned by art museums? No. We judge each piece by its own merit. That's what people need to do with POD books. There is no difference between artists selling their paintings and authors selling their books.

As for bookstores and libraries, it is hard to get POD books into both because it's hard to get their attention. Libraries are perfectly open to buying them if they're made aware of the book's existence and are interested. I've had my book picked up by a few libraries, though I have no idea how they were made aware of it. Bookstores on the other hand, are much harder to get into. Most bookstores only take books they can return. POD books are not returnable. Thus, the only way to get into a bookstore is to A. Stock the book yourself and take returns (a costly endeavor) or B. give them the book on consignment, which can work great locally.

Does POD publishing enable you more freedom on what you'll create, and does that translate for more choice for the reader?

Creative freedom is really what self-publishing is all about. And just like artists, some of us are just learning to sketch, while others are working on literary Sistine Chapels. It's a diverse group of creators. My hope is that POD would be seen as less of an arena for the previously rejected and more of a place for creative writers to express ideas and stories that have high merit, but may not be mainstream enough for traditional publishing.

In fact, I would recommend to any writer wanting to become a professional novelist to publish their first book through POD. There is no better learning experience. You'll learn what it takes to put a novel together. You'll learn about distribution, marketing, promotion and the best lesson a writer can learn before approaching a publisher—do complete strangers enjoy you're writing? You might learn that you need to go back to the drawing board, read through Strunk & White one more time and take a class or two...or you might just find your book is a best seller, snag an agent and have your book translated into multiple languages....it happens.

INTERVIEW FOR LULU.COM'S DECEMBER, 2005 NEWSLETTER

Your book is about the ramifications of time travel? If you could travel back in time, what would you go back and do?

The book isn't so much about the ramifications of time travel on time. It's more about the ramifications of time travel on the characters. The reason why time is unaffected is because, in opposition to popular fiction I have written the truth about time—it is fixed. It cannot be changed.

When I wrote the book my answer to "where would you have gone?" would have been the same as the main characters: the death and resurrection (or not) or Jesus Christ. Now, having learned a lesson about faith from the journey of my main character, I would choose something related but for different reasons: Moses parting the sea. This doesn't necessarily reflect a desire to see if it really happened or not, just that it would be a spectacular sight.

What made you decide to write *The Didymus Contingency*?

Basically, I was sitting on the couch, jotting story ideas (for screenplays, I wasn't writing novels at the time) in my notebook while watching Dexter's Laboratory. I basically asked myself the question which is the basis of the book, the same one you asked me, if I could go back in time, and witness any event, where would I go?

The answer I came up with was *The Didymus Contingency*, which was originally written as a screenplay (and was in development at one point) with the title, *Didymus*. I adapted the screenplay into a novel two years after writing the screenplay because I got the novel writing bug and knew that story had the widest appeal. I have since adapted three screenplays into novels.

Did you hire/use an editor?

I used an editor, but didn't have to hire one. This was my editing line-up for *Didymus*. Step one: Father-in-law. He's a whiz with typos. Step two: My editor (Lauren Rossini) at Lone Eagle Press, who published my first book, *The Screenplay Workbook*, edited *The Didymus Contingency* for free...she's good like that. Step three: My wife, Hilaree. She was an English major, a reader for an agency and has a keen eye for bad writing...and she's not afraid to tell me. Unlike most family, she won't say everything I write is great. If it's awful, she'll tell me. She even uses a red pen.

What is your favorite book?

This is actually a hard question to answer. It seems that every four or five books I read I discover a new favorite. Previous favorites include: Prey by Michael Crichton, Relic by Douglas Preston and Lincoln Child and Ice Hunt by James Rollins. Out of the bunch Rollins has probably influenced my writing more than the rest so

I'll give him the #1 spot with Deep Fathom. I'm a science based action/adventure junky.

Elvis or The Beatles? If Elvis, young or old? If The Beatles, Paul or John?

The Beatles. I can't say I'm a huge fan, but I do turn their songs up on the radio, and even sing along to a few. Elvis I can't stand. Paul or John? John...because I like the name better. I'm more of a Doors kind of guy...and James Brown. Elvis with his jutting lips and hips just kind of creeps me out.

What is your favorite holiday candy? For that matter, what's your favorite holiday?

Christmas is hands down my favorite holiday, though as an adult I'm seeing the decline of something that used to be magical. Now that I have a daughter I can rekindle some of that Christmas magic, but it's become so commercial and anxiety ridden that it's hard to focus on the real reason we celebrate the holiday at all...chocolate bon bons!

What inspires you? What is your secret for overcoming writer's block?

Getting out on a boat, exploring the ocean, feeling the mystery of what lurks beneath inspires me more than anything. On a day to day basis I'm inspired by good movies, books and…dare I say it, video games. Between writing chapters I typically play a half hour of one game or another. Today it was Star Wars Battlefront II (I beat it). But it's a poor substitute for the briny deep.

As for writer's block. A lot of people hate me for this. I never have it. Ever. I can sit down any time, any day and start writing. I generally day dream while I'm not writing (driving, in the shower, changing a diaper) so when I sit down to write I'm good to go. I typically have a backlog of several chapters in my head waiting to be put on the page. Even when I finish a book, I'm ready with the next. I'm 60 pages into my fifth novel now, but I'm also researching and outlining the sixth. I think this was developed through my art background (I was an illustration major in college). Many people have a fear of the blank page—in writing and in art. I've always adored the blank page because it allows me to set my captive imagination free.

When you first had the idea, what moved you more, the sci-fi angle? Or the religious aspect?

I've always been a product of science fiction. I was raised on Dr. Who, Battlestar Galactica and Star Trek. Everything I write has some aspect of science fiction to it. But with *The Didymus Contingency* the science is really a vehicle to reach the religious story. That doesn't mean it's not science fiction, the story couldn't exist without the science, but the plot isn't driven by the science.

Word is that you landed an agent after this, how did having your book on Lulu help or hinder that?

Lulu, in short, made signing with an agent a reality. Here's basically how it went down. I put my book together, released it on Lulu and got the global distribution package. About midway through the second month the book exploded. It hit the Barnes&Noble.com bestseller list (let's say on Tuesday—I don't remember what day it was) and on Wednesday I get an e-mail from an agency* that I and most serious writers have heard of. A large percentage of their authors are NY Times bestsellers. The agent asked me to send him the book, which I did the next day. On Monday, four days later, the agent called and offered to represent me. I accepted of course. Now he's taking it out to the large publishing houses and we've got Bulgarian and Romanian translation deals.

>   *I'm not currently giving the agency's name out because when I do I get a flurry of requests for me to send them other author's books. Being the new guy at the agency, I'm hardly in a position to do so.

What's the most uncannily accurate shot you've ever made at an inanimate object with a stone?

Let's see...there was that one time I hit my childhood neighbor's window...actually, I did that a few times, but it was an accident I swear. I'm thinking now. I'm remembering a lot of times when I shot them in a slingshot, launched them from a homemade catapult or hit them with a bat...but threw...ah! I've got it.

Upon spying a hornet's nest I decided it would be a good idea to hurl rocks at it with a friend. It was in a bush and we assumed the bush needles and a twenty foot gap would give us time to make our escape. My first shot tore through the nest's outer husk and, well, stirred up a hornet's nest. The event taught me one important lesson. When you throw rocks at a hornet's nest always bring a friend who runs slower than you. Seven stings taught him to never throw rocks at a wasp's nest. It's funny how two different people can experience the same thing yet learn two completely different lessons. True story.

Any advice for Lulu authors, or those considering self-publishing?

I've got plenty, but the #1 piece of advice I give (if your goal is to land a traditional publisher, find an agent or sell a boatload of books) is to publish a professional book. Make sure it's edited professionally. Make sure the cover and back cover are indistinguishable from the other books being sold in stores. And most of all, don't fool yourself into believing you're ready to be published if you're not. It's better to find out before people are spending $18 for your book, because if you still need practice, they're going to let you and the rest of the world know about it. Get your ego mutilated in private before letting the public have a go at you. Find honest people to read your work, preferably strangers or hired professionals.

However, if your goal is to have fun or view the whole thing as a learning experience, by all means publish what you've got. Though it is much more painful to have your work critiqued by angry readers, there is also no quicker way to learn what or where you need to improve. Even with all the success *The Didymus Contingency* has had and hopefully will continue to have, there are critics out there. But I'm thankful for them. They're only helping me improve.

10

FINAL THOUGHTS

Not every POD book can be successful. To believe so may leave you severely disappointed. Your mindset when publishing via POD should be realistic. You may become a bestseller. You may just as easily not sell more than 10 copies. What you must also realize is that this is the case with all authors, POD or traditionally published. It's a hit or miss business. So many authors have their first book traditionally published, only to sell scant amounts of books, and be dropped.

What makes POD more challenging is that you're not only competing with the big publishers, but you're also fighting the

POD stigma. As author and publisher, you have the opportunity to control everything about your book. The responsibility for every aspect of the final outcome rests squarely on your shoulders. If the book fails...and I fret to say this...it is your fault and your fault alone.

Once you've stopped drawing horns on the picture of me on the About the Author page, please read this carefully. I've mentioned that you are author, publisher, designer, marketer and editor. If there is a reason, whether it be a bad cover, crummy editing, non-existent promotion or a lousy story, there is no one to blame but yourself. This is one of the benefits to being traditionally published. If things don't pan out the way you dreamed, you can't blame the bad cover or point the finger at an editor who should've found the flaws in your writing.

But you're alone in this endeavor. If something slips through the cracks, they're your cracks. Even if you hire an editor or a graphic designer to do the cover, these things are done to your satisfaction. You are the one giving the final approval and it's your ego on the line when you publish your work. Do yourself a favor and do the work. Get the book right and then promote the heck out of it. It doesn't take a lot of money, as you've seen, but it does take a lot of time, energy and brutal honesty.

Even as I write the ending to this book, I'm unsure of how it will be received. I believe it's a useful book. I wish I had it when I first published my POD book. But please remember, even if you follow everything thing I've done, even if you learn from my mistakes, if your book isn't as good as it should be (and could be) failure, bad reviews and embarrassment loom ahead.

I hate stories with a depressing ending, but all this doom and gloom serves a purpose. I want to encourage all the POD People publishing today and in the future to only publish quality work. It's the only way to get the results you want. It's the only way to sell books. It's the only way to get an agent's or publisher's attention. Rushing the job just to see your name on a book is foolish.

If you're one of the many POD People who have published a book already and have seen it struggle to get noticed, here's my advice. Remove the book. If you've already spent a chunk of change on a global package somewhere, accept the loss as money well spent on an important lesson. You will do better to rewrite the book, have it edited, put some real effort into the cover and re-publish at a later date. You must also consider the possibility that this particular book just shouldn't be published. I've written several screenplays that I can look back on now and say, "That story is crap!" At the time I fully believed it was great, but I was wrong. You may also be too attached to your story to see its flaws. If you think this might be true, remove it, set it aside and write another book. Given time, as you learn the craft and the publishing business, you might come to understand what you had done wrong.

Even though *The Didymus Contingency* has sold thousands of books, has been picked up by an agent, is being translated into multiple languages and has received countless wonderful reviews, I still wonder if it's good enough.

Why hasn't it been picked up by a domestic publisher yet?

Will it ever be?

Will I ever sell 10,000 copies?

Is there something I can do to increase sales even more?

Will my agent drop the book?

Will my other three novels be as well received?

Should I put out a second edition and correct the few typos?

I have become my own biggest critic. I still fume about missing the chance of getting pre-publication reviews. I continue to wonder what would have happened if I went with IUniverse (I would have qualified for their star program and could have been sold in physical stores) instead of Lulu. I'm not a self-loathing monster; I know I did more right than I did wrong. The success of *The Didymus Contingency* is proof of that. But because I'm honest about the quality of my writing, about the mistakes I've made and the challenges I face, I feel confident I will only improve as an author.

The path to finding a traditional publisher and making the big bucks may take a while longer, even years. When I decided to be a writer I knew the path existed, but had no idea how long it would be. I've seen the end within reach a few times only to backtrack time and again. But things are not hopeless. As we POD People improve our books and sales, the stigma will fade and the world will take note. Until then, be honest, patient, and steadfast.

11

THE PODs

There are tons of choices when looking into PODs. So many it can be disconcerting. But I know one of the main concerns POD People face is money. This is why many of us begin the search for a POD service, because we're poor starving artists. This was one of my top criteria. Thus, I have listed as many POD services as I could scrounge up (there are a lot) and listed what their cheapest option is. That means it is their base program, offering the most limited amount of services. Take the time to figure out which is your best match. If there is no possible way you can create a cover, you might look into finding a service that bundles a cover design into the price. The same is true for marketing services, interior layout and editing. But I highly recommend doing these things your-self. Even if your book flops, at least you'll have learned something from the experience. In addition, you'll probably find it cheaper to hire an editor and graphic artist. It's also more likely that the qual-ity will be better than if you use a POD service's in house (and of-ten pricey) offerings. Most POD covers, created by individuals or the POD services themselves, aren't really worth writing home about.

I'm sure the pricing changes frequently, so please forgive me if the numbers don't match up when you pay them a visit.

Lulu.com

I know what you're thinking, "L isn't the first letter of the alpha-bet!" Well, you're right, but if you're looking for a POD, Lulu.com should be the first place you look. I could be biased by my incredi-ble experience with them, but you'll notice their most expensive option is lower then the cheapest option of every other POD ser-vice. That alone deems them worthy of consideration.

Cheapest Option: $34.95

Most Expensive Option: $150

Authorhouse

www.authorhouse.com

Cheapest Option: $698

Advantage Books

www.advbooks.com

Cheapest Option: $999

Biblio Books

www.bibliobooks.com,

Cheapest Option: $1,450

Book Locker

www.booklocker.com

Cheapest Option: $217

Book Surge

www.booksurge.com

Cheapest Option: $498

Cold Tree Press

www.coldtreepress.com

Cheapest Option: $900

Cork Hill Press

www.corkhillpress.com

Cheapest Option: $500

Dog Ear Publishing

www.dogearpublishing.com

Cheapest Option: $699

eBookstand

www.ebookstand.com

Cheapest Option: $979

E-BookTime

www.e-booktime.com

Cheapest Option: $395

Elderberry Press

www.elderberrypress.com

Cheapest Option: $5,500+$0.02/per word

Foremost Press

www.foremostpress.com

Cheapest Option: $397

Golden Pillar Publishing

www.goldenpillarpublishing.com

Cheapest Option: $500

Global Authors Publications

www.globalauthorspublications.com

Cheapest Option: $1,000

HelioGraphica

www.heliographica.com,

Cheapest Option: $299

IndyPublish

www.indypublish.com

Cheapest Option: $189

Infinity Publishing

www.infinitypublishing.com

Cheapest Option: $499

Inkwater Press

www.inkwaterpress.com

Cheapest Option: $899

iUniverse

www.iuniverse.com,

Cheapest Option: $450

Llumina

www.llumina.com

Cheapest Option: $699

My Life My Words

www.mylifemywords.com

Cheapest Option: $265

Outskirts Press

www.outskirtspress.com

Cheapest Option: $399

Prairie View Publishing

www.prairieviewpublishing.com

Cheapest Option: $450

Press Forward

www.pressforward.com

Cheapest Option: $370

PABD

www.pabd.com

Cheapest Option: $445

Trafford Publishing

www.trafford.com

Cheapest Option: $990

Virtualbookworm Publishing

www.virtualbookworm.com

Cheapest Option: $495

Xlibris

www.xlibris.com

Cheapest Option: $900

Your Own World Books

www.yowbooks.com

Cheapest Option: $495

"How many a man has thrown up his hands at a time when a little more effort, a little more patience would have achieved success?"

Elbert Hubbard

ABOUT THE AUTHOR

Photograph by Tom Mungovan

JEREMY ROBINSON was born in Beverly, Massachusetts in 1974. He stayed in Beverly through college, attending Gordon College and Montserrat College of Art. His writing career began in 1995 and includes stints on comic books, and thirteen completed screenplays, several of which have been produced, optioned or have gone into development. He is the author of *The Screenplay Workbook* and several published short stories and articles including *The Difference between Science Fiction and Fantasy* for *Script Magazine*. *The Didymus Contingency*, his first published novel was published via print-on-demand and quickly became a bestseller.

He currently resides in New Hampshire with his wife, Hilaree and daughter, Aquila...and one more (Solomon) on the way!

He can be reached via the web at www.jeremyrobinsononline.com or directly at info@jeremyrobinsononline.com.

Printed in the United States
72992LV00004B/58

9 780978 655105